The Politics Of City And State Bureaucracy

THE POLITICS OF CITY AND STATE BUREAUCRACY

DOUGLAS M. FOX

GOODYEAR PUBLISHING COMPANY, INC.
Pacific Palisades, California

Copyright © 1974
GOODYEAR PUBLISHING COMPANY, INC.
Pacific Palisades, California

Current printing (last digit):
10 9 8 7 6 5 4 3 2 1

ISBN: 0-87620-711-5
Library of Congress Catalog Card Number: 73-79754
Y: 7115-2

Printed in the United States of America

For my family: Linda, Jeffrey, and Marcia

Contents

Preface

This introduction to the political dynamics of sub-national bureaucracy in the United States is intended primarily as a textbook for college under-graduates. It is my hope, however, that other types of readers will look at this book, and let me know their opinion of it. This is a slim volume, largely because of the paucity of literature in the field. I would greatly appreciate being informed of relatively esoteric literature-publications of university bureaus of government research and public administration, un-published papers, theses, dissertations, in-house and consultant studies, and the like which I have missed. In addition, I welcome criticism of any argu-ments made in the book. I would like to expand the volume from an exploratory effort to a more definitive account of the subject. To do so, I will need all the help I can get, and I thank readers who take the trouble to help me.

I am happy to acknowledge the assistance of the following persons who have greatly contributed to improvements upon early drafts of this book. Because I often refused their advice, however, all shortcomings are my own. My greatest debt is to the late Wallace S. Sayre. It was Professor Sayre who first stirred my interest in bureaucratic politics. His students will note the stamp of his influence on every page of this book, even though he did not read the manuscript. Profound thanks are due to Robert S. Gilmour, Harold Seidman, and Deil S. Wright, who carefully reviewed the manuscript and did not balk at telling me where changes had to be made. Others who read all or part of the manuscript and provided many helpful comments, for which I am grateful, are Timothy Campbell, George Cole, Leo V. Donohue, Edward Dowling, Nanette Gilmour, Bill Johnson, Fred Kort, Jack Krauskopf, Rosaline Levenson, Morgan McGinley, Albert Schukoske, Bruce Stave, and Morton Tenzer. Frances Stearns did an excellent job of typing the manuscript, while special thanks are due Betty Seaver, who not only typed several drafts of the manuscript, but did her best to improve my prose style. Last but far from least, Goodyear editors Gail Weingart and David Grady, with whom it was a pleasure to work, made the final stages of manuscript preparation almost a pleasure.

Introduction

Off-duty police picket city hall and boo the mayor.

Teachers go out on strike.

State welfare workers meet to denounce the policies of the governor and his welfare commissioner.

Newspaper stories similar to these have probably appeared by now in most American newspapers and on television news programs. Such incidents indicate that government employees are a political force in their own right, not merely the pawns of elected government officials. Yet the study of bureaucratic politics remains curiously underdeveloped as we approach the end of the twentieth century. Political science textbooks concentrate on the legislature, the chief executive, the party system, and interest groups. The bureaucracy, if it is mentioned at all, is subordinate. These books reflect the literature in political science, which is notably deficient in its treatment of the bureaucracy. As one study has noted:

> The decisive transformation of modern government has been the growth in scope and power of government bureaucracy and the consequent problems which have been posed for the viability of democratic party politics. . . . It is striking to note the extent to which contemporary political behavior research focuses on the election process to the exclusion of the administrative arena of power.[1]

Neglect of bureaucratic politics is especially notable in the literature on urban and state politics. Many works purporting to deal with the politics of a given state say nothing about its bureaucracy, which leads one to ponder—and perhaps envy—the experience of authors to whom state government bureaucracy is irrelevant. Two political scientists have remarked that "even though it is generally recognized that most key decisions are initiated or made within executive agencies, the conditions under which they operate . . . remain unmapped and challenges for future students of state politics."[2]

The author must acknowledge, then, the extent to which this book is an exploratory and tentative effort. There is not a single conclusion herein about the power of various political participants that is based on over-

1

whelming evidence. What this book does is report what is known and suggest subjects for future researchers to investigate. There is an almost bewildering variety of patterns of bureaucratic behavior, but the causes of this variety are not yet known. When more data are assembled, understanding will increase.

BUREAUCRACY ON THE MARCH

The observation that man lives in a world of large organizations to which he must increasingly conform is a truism. It is a fundamental fact of human existence today, one that will not go away. Rather, the growth of these organizations is steady. In the period 1950–1972, for example, employees of urban and state governments in the United States increased from four million to over ten million—almost one-eighth of the total labor force. The rate of increase far outstripped the growth rate of the national economy or the national population. We live more and more in a world of organization men. Doctors who once practiced from one-man offices now form group practices; college professors who formerly scorned any hint of collective action join unions; one has difficulty finding a lawyer outside a firm; and research teams have replaced the individual scientist. All of these changes reflect the growing complexity and interdependence of modern technological society. While these observations are hardly novel, they are crucial to an understanding of the nature of modern government and the kinds of control that political actors can exercise over the executive branch.

In recent years Americans have been told that the United States faces a number of crises—urban, racial, ecological, economic, drug-related, and so on. Any problem solving in these areas must be accomplished by administrative agencies, whether public or private. People from all walks of life are disenchanted with the performance of today's bureaucracies, as angry confrontations between parents and striking teachers, welfare mothers' organizations and social workers, and minority group representatives and police bear out; but elimination of the bureaucracies is impossible. Instead, the only option for those desiring change is to try to make the bureaucracies behave in a manner different from their current mode of operation. Bureaucrats are going to solve or fail to solve the urban crisis or any other crisis, because they are the actors involved in the implementation of programs designed to solve problems.

Further, it is bureaucrats at the state and urban levels who must work on the most pressing domestic problems. There is a good deal of rhetoric about the growth of the federal government, but a look at the federal system supports the contention that state and urban governments are just as important in the realm of domestic policy. Indeed, it is difficult to find areas of human behavior in which city and state agencies are not active. A partial list of functions includes law enforcement, mass transportation, welfare, health, education, regulation of business and other groups, environmental protection, housing, and land-use planning. The three million civilian federal employees equal the number of state government employees, while there are seven million employees of local governments.[3] The growth rate of state and urban government personnel far exceeded that of federal government or private business personnel in the decade 1960–1970, and it should continue to accelerate in the 1970s. In fiscal year 1972, state and local governments spent slightly more money raised through their own revenue systems on domestic programs than did the federal government. When federal grant programs are added to state and local budgets, however, one can see why the lower levels of government have so many more employees than do the higher levels. In fiscal year 1969, for example, almost 70 percent of the funds spent on domestic programs was spent at the state and local levels—where the "action" of domestic programs is centered. Thus, we are looking not at declining institutions but at one of the most dynamic sectors of American society.

DEFINITIONS AND CONCEPTS

The use of words such as "politics" and "bureaucracy" necessitates a precise definition of terms. In this book *politics* is synonymous with the governmental policy-making process, while *partisan politics*—the usual colloquial conception of the term—is only one aspect of politics. Any person or group involved in the policy-making process is a political *actor*, not because he is a frustrated thespian, but because he behaves or acts in a way intended to influence the outcome of the process.

Here *bureaucrats* are defined as employees of the executive branch of government, and the term does not have the negative connotations typically associated with its usage in everyday speech; *bureaucracy* consists of all organizations and personnel in the executive branch. Throughout the book neither term is used in other than a descriptive way.

Some other definitions relevant to bureaucracy are also in order. A *line agency* is an agency designated the task of carrying out such operations of government as urban renewal, health care, and transportation. Within line agencies are found personnel dealing with *staff* functions, or functions necessary to maintain the agency, rather than the actual implementation of programs. Both the chief and a budget analyst within the financial management division of a state mental health department, for example, perform staff functions, while the doctors and nurses dealing with patients perform line functions. An *overhead agency* is a central staff agency with no line functions—for example, central budget, management, personnel, and auditing agencies that assist the chief executive or legislature in the supervision of line agencies.

The term *department* refers to a formally organized cluster of bureaus (a department of transportation may include bureaus dealing with high-ways, air travel, railroads, and water travel); a *bureau* is a subunit of a department and is typically the basic building block of the bureaucracy, especially as the department increases in size. The word *agency* is used as a generic term synonymous with both bureau and department. While *chief executives* are the officials who have the greatest amount of formal authority in the executive branch in their governmental jurisdiction, *political executives* are secondary top officials, typically department heads, who are elected or appointed by the chief executive and/or other government officials.

The mode of organization of this book is bureaucentric. Each political actor surveyed is observed in relation to bureaus and their policies and programs. In the examination of bureau-actor relationships, an attempt is made to propose some tentative answers to the question of which actors are most powerful under which kinds of circumstances. In this case it is necessary to distinguish between two types of policy-making phases: first, what is here called *policy development;* and second, *policy implementation.* Policy development refers to the process in which a new authoritative regulation is enacted by the executive branch, the legislature, the courts, or an actor formally designated with the necessary authority, such as an agency head or bureau chief. Policy development is embodied in new written authoritative regulations rather than informal norms of behavior in government. Thus, examples of policy development include an executive order from the governor or mayor, a statute from the legislature, a regulation issued by an agency head, and a ruling from the judiciary. Whether the new policy represents a major or only an incremental change is of no importance; what is of consequence in this definition is a recognition that this is a new policy embodied in a formal and explicit authoritative act of a government agency.

Policy implementation, on the other hand, refers to the process by which the policies resulting from the policy development process are actually enforced or carried out. In some cases agencies may issue more-detailed regulations to guide staff in the execution of the policy development order. The policy implementation process, however, may not involve any formal promulgation of new regulations. Policy implementation is as important as policy development, because the regulations produced in the policy development process are not self-enforcing. Some examples should clarify the point. All large American cities have housing and building codes of different types, certain sections of which subject landlords to penalties if they do not maintain property at a level adequate to safeguard basic standards of health. The regulations, however, must be enforced by building inspectors, and the gap between the mandate of the law and the actual practice is a large one. Generally, inspection agencies do not have staffs large enough to perform their police function. Further, inspectors may look with sympathy on the position of landlords and may not make major efforts to get them to remedy code violations. In some cases the leniency may be due to "presents" from the landlords; in other cases, it may simply be due to the prevailing norms of the agency, which may be unsympathetic to slum tenants and thus beneficial to landlords. Another example is that of court decisions requiring police to inform arrested suspects of their constitutional rights before undergoing interrogation. It is the police, not the courts, who decide whether or not they are going to follow these edicts.

It is important to make the distinction between policy development and policy implementation, because the power of different actors may vary, depending upon which of the two phases of the policy-making process they participate in. For this reason, both stages of the policy-making process are discussed in each chapter. This dichotomy better enables one to answer the central questions around which this book is organized: What power do different kinds of bureaucrats have to affect public policy? What variations in this power are found among different governments and issue areas, and what causes these differences in power? What power do other participants in politics have relative to the bureaucracy? What variations are found, and why?

Conclusion

Bureaucrats have become not only the key problem-solvers of our time, but powerful figures in the political system. Bureaucratic growth has occurred most rapidly at the state and local levels of government in the United States, and this book examines the power of bureaucrats at those levels to affect public policy.

CHAPTER ONE

Administrative Agencies and Bureaucrats

Although most Americans seem to like to make generalizations about bureaucrats and bureaucratic behavior, there are in fact many disparate types of bureaucrats and bureaus that differ greatly in behavior. In this chapter some of the principal types of bureau and bureaucratic orientations and their relationship to bureaucratic power are discussed.

BUREAUCRATIC CULTURE

Every administrative agency has its own culture which gives it a unique identity. This culture, or value system, reflects the agency's goals. Understanding the nature of bureaucratic culture is necessary to appreciate the political behavior of a bureau. Although it is possible to generalize about bureaucratic behavior, one must always be cognizant of the enormous variations in culture and action that distinguish one bureau from another.

There are two main kinds of agency goals: those relating to agency programs, and those relating to maintenance of the agency as an organization. While most agencies are probably concerned with both, there are notable dissimilarities in the degree of commitment to each goal.

Agencies whose members are recruited on a patronage basis, that is, hired because of their support for the political party in power, are unlikely to have much interest in program goals. Patronage-based public works departments, for example, are less concerned about the nature of state or community building projects than about making sure that their party stays in power and that the agency's payroll is not reduced. Members of such agencies are more interested in keeping their jobs than in deciding which lighting system to recommend. This is not to say that individuals are inattentive to such matters, but rather that these individuals are only occasional exceptions to the predominant bureau culture. Such bureaus are one type of organization-maintenance agency.

Much wider variation in goals is found among agencies under a merit system. The merit system, or civil service, differs from the patronage system in requiring successful performance on examinations for entry and promotion. After serving a probationary period, the employee secures tenure in the system, which means that he cannot be removed without cause and that he is entitled to a hearing if an attempt is made to dismiss him for cause. If the agency's budget is cut, and his position with it, he is entitled to transfer to any equivalent position that may exist elsewhere in the agency. While all merit systems share these formal characteristics, the ways in which they are interpreted and administered differ. Employees may be evaluated for promotion primarily by written examinations, or by evaluation of job performance. Employees may respond to job classification systems by balking at all tasks not included in their job descriptions, or by acting in a more flexible manner.

In merit systems stressing written examinations for promotion and a rigid job classification, bureaucrats are likely to behave as caricatures of themselves. That is, since they function in a system in which performance has little relation to promotion, they may be more concerned with protesting the perquisites of their positions, being promoted, and doing only the necessary work than with achieving program goals. The New York City personnel system, for example, seems to have functioned in this manner for some time.[1] Although some program-oriented bureaucrats exist in such a culture, they are a minority, exceptions to the norm.

Program-oriented bureaus are much less likely to stress written examinations for promotion, because such behavior almost precludes achievement of program goals, whether they be reduction in drug addiction, increased tax collection rates, or expansion of higher education. To reach program goals, it is necessary to reward goal-oriented individuals and give them leeway. All program-oriented bureaus manifest varying degrees of commitment to maintenance of the organization and job security. No "pure" program-oriented bureaus exist, any more than do "pure" organization-maintenance bureaus. The differences are in degree, and it may often be difficult to discern whether a bureau is primarily program- or survival-oriented.

The personnel systems of program-oriented bureaus are not all the same. One may give outsiders with comparable experience elsewhere middle-management positions; another may reserve such posts for those already with the bureau. One may encourage personnel exchanges with other bureaus; another may bar them. One may allow individuals from a number of backgrounds equal entry opportunity; another may restrict entry to narrowly specified groups. Bureaus that follow exclusionary practices in recruitment of personnel are more likely to be rigid in their preferred means of achieving program goals, while agencies that admit different kinds of new blood are more likely to be flexible in this regard.

The groups that an agency favors in recruitment provide a clue to agency orientation. Some agencies have long favored certain ethnic groups; in northeastern cities, for example, the Irish are disproportionately represented in many police departments, while in New York City, Italians have been drawn to the sanitation department, Jews to the schools, and Negroes to the health department. There is sufficient evidence to indicate that these recruitment patterns result in different treatment both for citizens served by the agency and for employees outside the dominant group.

Lower-class minority children, for instance, may be considered unteachable by the middle-class nonminority teacher, and they may thus be fated to be dropouts.[2]   Likewise, some Negroes may not bother to try for promotion within the New York City Department of Education because they believe they have no chance for promotion.

Professionals are another type of group that may dominate bureau personnel systems. Frederick Mosher defines a profession as "a reasonably clear-cut occupational field, which ordinarily requires higher education at least through the bachelor's degree, and which offers a lifetime career to its members."[3]   Professionals thus include teachers, engineers, and social workers, as well as what Mosher calls "emergent" professions—personnel specialists, financial managers, police, and assessors, among others—hoping to gain recognition as professional groups. It may in fact be necessary to be a member of a profession to gain an executive position in some agencies. One may even have to have been graduated from a certain school to be in the running for top posts in a state parks and forest bureau or a department of education. Such professionally dominated agencies may be especially inflexible in a changing situation because the profession normally has a well-articulated ideology built up over the years to justify its program orientation.[4]   Attempts to criticize or change the ideology are resisted by those who have advanced in such a system. One example is the social work profession, which still continues to stress service to individual clients, while critics within and outside the profession argue that group political action is a more suitable solution to poverty.

Feelings of "professionalism" have grown to a point where today the employees of almost any agency refer to themselves as professionals and their jobs as professions. One characteristic of this professionalism is a determination to keep the personnel system's rules unchanged so that other types of people cannot enter. Policemen, for example, resist rule changes such as reduction of the minimum height and formal education requirements that would allow more Spanish-Americans to enter the system. Opposition to change is always justified in the name of professionalism and quality, to be sure, but more notable is the attempt to preserve the existing bureaucratic culture.[5]

Junior bureaucrats go through an informal "socialization" process after entering an agency; that is, they are exposed to and assume the norms of the bureaucratic culture. If the junior bureaucrat deviates markedly from these norms, he is likely to have a difficult time. For example, he may be assigned to the less interesting and important tasks of the bureau and may not be promoted as quickly. If a bureau has a culture that its employees strongly support, the deviant is unlikely to last long. If there are different "camps" within the bureau, with no single, dominant culture, the deviant may be able to stay; but unless he adheres to some bureaucratic subculture, his career chances within the bureau will be very limited.[6]

Subcultures, or competing belief systems, are more likely to exist in agencies that are more "open" to outsiders. Some state departments of community or urban affairs seem to fit this pattern, as do many newly created agencies. While the existence of subcultures may indicate diversity and flexibility, it can also cause problems for a bureau, such as internal conflict and lack of goal consensus. Black policemen, for example, often have their own union or professional association and often differ with their white colleagues on such crucial issues as treatment of minority group suspects.[7] Functionally similar departments may have markedly different program goals, even though their personnel systems share the same norms.

Is a fire department, for instance, more concerned with fire prevention than with putting out fires; vice versa; or concerned equally with both? Two departments with identical personnel system norms may have different policy orientations, which may be caused by the interest group politics of their city (those desiring the best fire protection versus those wanting lowest costs for government) or by strong individual departmental leaders committed to certain programs. The police chief of Miami Beach, for example, took a much less hard-line approach to demonstrators at the 1972 national party conventions than did his Chicago counterpart in 1968. By intensive educational and indoctrination programs, the Miami Beach chief was able to avoid the bloody confrontations that took place in Chicago. Studies have shown that police department orientations differ greatly, some being based on rigid enforcement of the law, others on maintenance of order and willingness to forego arrest procedures if a family dispute or possible riot can thus be avoided.[8]

Some bureaus are anxious to expand their programs, others are content to continue as they have in the past, and still others—admittedly few—may be relatively unconcerned as they fade away. The degree to which agencies are oriented in these directions lends infinite complexity to the theme of bureau variety.[9]

One crucial factor distinguishing bureaucratic cultures relates to the nature of the work performed by the bureau and the groups with which bureaucrats interact. One writer has distinguished "street-level" bureaucrats—those who directly interact with citizens, have considerable discretion in carrying out their jobs, and have great impact on citizens—from other bureaucrats.[10] Police, teachers, and welfare workers fall into this category, and they differ from many bureaucrats who interact primarily with large institutions, whether public (other bureaus, at their own or different levels of government) or private (corporations or labor unions). This distinction goes a long way towards distinguishing municipal from state and federal bureaus. Bureaucrats above the city level are much more likely to interact with local government officials and officials of private institutions than are municipal bureaucrats who have a greater proportion of street-level bureaucrats in their ranks. City government is where the action is, because it is where citizens have face-to-face contact with bureaucrats. As a result, it is no surprise that the intensity of conflict generated at the municipal level exceeds that at the state level. Here angry confrontations over school policy between teachers' unions and minority groups, clashes between welfare mothers' groups and social workers, and protests against the police are not unusual, while at higher levels of government such conflicts rarely occur.

These differences are reflected in bureau cultures. City employee unions are more militant and aggressive in making demands than are their state counterparts, in part because they feel more endangered by the hostile environment in which they function. The greater frequency of government union strikes at the city level can be explained by environment and its effect on bureau culture.

In recent years, there has been a significant increase in the number of government employees who belong to unions. Such a development was a shock to many leaders of the civil service reform movement, because they believed that unions would be unnecessary under the merit system. However, the increase in union ranks indicates that merit systems do not answer all the felt needs of government employees.

In the 1960s, for the first time, strikes by government employees became commonplace. Previously, strikes not only had been outlawed, but had been perceived by most government employees as illegitimate. Today, however, it is not a question of whether government employees unions will lead their members out on strike, but which union will go out next. Strikes in such vital areas as sanitation and mass transit are no longer unusual. In addition, many unions that have never gone out on strike engage in "job actions," which are designed to put pressure on city governments. These typically take the form of some kind of work slowdown, accomplished by members calling in sick—police get the "blue flu"—or performing their duties at a much more leisurely pace. Government employees' unions are well organized and fully capable of relatively drastic action when they feel such action is necessary to protect their interests.[11]

Union activity reinforces a bureau's culture, for a union is interested in the welfare of its members, not the welfare of potential members. Thus, unions act to achieve an assured role in making the policies that become the agency's work. Be they police or social workers, bureaucrats seek policies that suit their tradition and aspirations. New York City firemen stress fighting fires rather than fire prevention, and they resist attempts to change this emphasis.[12] Further, unions wish to control the procedures under which bureaucrats work. This is done to insure that there be as little disturbance as possible of routines and regulations, personnel systems, and grievance procedures. Many unions today not only are concerned with employee conditions and grievances, but act to attain a voice for their members in bureau policy development: teacher unions have opposed school decentralization, while welfare workers have argued for the right to join the commissioner in setting agency policy.[13]

While these generalizations about bureaucratic behavior are normally accurate, one should be careful not to take them too literally. Although bureaucrats are usually conservative, in that they tend to oppose change in bureau procedures, personnel systems, and programs, there are bureaucrats who wish to make changes. Those in the antipoverty program have fought a running battle in recent years with bureaucrats in older agencies. Legal services program lawyers, for example, often sue welfare departments on behalf of their clients. While it is difficult to determine whether bureaus with one type of culture are more powerful than bureaus with another, knowledge of bureau culture can give insights into the goals and tactics a bureau is likely to pursue. In this way it is possible to determine what kind of political participation characterizes a bureau with a certain type of culture, even though its chances for success cannot be predicted.

ADMINISTRATIVE STRUCTURE

The most striking feature of governmental structure at any level in the United States is fragmentation. Division and separation, rather than co-ordination and control, characterize American government. At the city, state, and federal levels, one finds a host of administrative agencies, rather than one department, carrying out related functional tasks. Fragmentation causes both duplication of effort and failure to act in some policy areas. In Connecticut, for example, recent attempts to establish day-care centers have been stymied because of the inability of the state departments of health, welfare, education, and community affairs—all of which have juris-diction over individual aspects of the program—to coordinate their efforts. As is ordinarily the case, all four departments were loath to give up one iota of authority. If they were to do so, all or many of their programs could presumably be taken away and located in another agency at a later date under similar circumstances. For this reason coordination must be achieved by forces outside the bureaus.[14]

One cause of fragmentation is the constitutional separation of the execu-tive and legislative branches. At all levels of government the chief executive and the legislature share administrative authority. This constitutional pat-tern may be more important than any other factor in explaining the frag-mented nature of American governmental bureaucracy, but constitutional provisions alone could not insure the continuance of fragmented govern-ment in the United States were it not for other sources of support in the political culture.

Long before independence from Great Britain, the colonial legislatures had feuded intensely with the governors appointed by the monarch. Out of this experience of antagonism toward the chief executive came the typical administrative structure of state and local government. Both mayors and governors were essentially figureheads in the period up to the American Civil War, since they had little power to veto legislation, to make appointments to and removals from administrative positions, and to participate in budgetary formulation. Not content with superiority over the chief executive, local and state legislatures usually structured their governments to provide the greatest possible fragmentation. Similar and overlapping functions were assigned not to a department but to separate and relatively autonomous agencies, answerable to no one but the legislature. The heads of these bureaus were often elected independently of the chief executive. Many bureaus were run by commissions whose members were appointed by the chief executive for fixed, staggered terms, subject to the consent of the legislature, and who were not subject to removal.

The political significance of fragmented government is that administrative agencies are insured a great deal of autonomy as political actors. Fragmentation makes it impossible for the chief executive—be he governor, mayor, or manager—to exercise centralized and coordinated control of the agencies nominally under his command. Since legislatures are unable to be administrative managers, the agencies in such a structure are, in a very real sense, on their own.

In the twentieth century, agency autonomy gained additional strength from the administrative reform movement. This movement, which was responsible for sweeping changes in the structure of American government in the late nineteenth and early twentieth centuries, was led by middle- and upper-class professionals and businessmen who were determined to root out the graft, corruption, and favoritism then endemic to government. The reformers believed that government should serve a generalized public interest rather than respond to special or political party demands.[15]

The reform movement exacerbated fragmentation by insisting that certain agencies be taken "out of politics," that is, be given a great deal of legal autonomy from the rest of the governmental structure. Such action was recommended by reformers after cases of blatant corruption and favoritism in agencies and after political interference in agency policy by the legislature or other actors. Education is a ubiquitous example of this kind of autonomy, whether the agency be a local school system or a state institution of higher education. The personnel systems of educational agencies are usually separate from the general state or city government personnel systems, and educational institutions enjoy a good deal of fiscal autonomy, in some areas enjoying the authority to raise revenues themselves. The reformers believed that policy (what has here been called policy development) could and should be rigorously separated from administration (here called policy implementation). The job of elected officeholders and the commissions and agency heads they appointed was to make policy, according to the reformers, while the job of the bureaucrat was to carry out the policy. Policy and administration were two separate fields, and meddling by politicians in administration or by bureaucrats in policy led to inefficient, corrupt government. The bureaucrat was pictured as a neutral implementer of any policy decided on by politicians.

Wiser heads knew then that this kind of rigid separation was impossible, and today very few people believe in the policy-administration dichotomy. Politics cannot be removed from administration any more than it can be from policy making. The distinction made in this book between policy development and policy implementation recognizes this fact. The distinction is made because patterns of political influence often differ in these two areas of policy making, not because they are totally different types of activity. Indeed, it is sometimes difficult to tell where development leaves off and implementation begins.

While the reformers designed civil service to take the politics out of administration, what they actually did was provide a new type of political actor. The attitude of bureaucrats toward fragmentation and the merit system varies by type of agency. Patronage employees naturally oppose a merit system, unless they are guaranteed a place in it. Merit system employees in line departments usually support both fragmentation and the civil service. The former ensures a degree of independence for their agency, while the latter gives them job security and reinforces the bureau culture.

Employees of professionalized agencies today are in fact the chief supporters of structural bureau autonomy.[16] Attempts by a chief executive to consolidate all line agencies under his control are met by criticism from bureaus and their interest group allies, who accuse him of treating their programs in a "political" manner, and who may launch campaigns to enlist opposition. Does the governor want to exert more control over the state university, or the mayor over the city health department? Then, according to the professionals in each agency, he is acting in a way that will weaken the agency in its attempt to achieve its program goals, and attacking or using the agency for his "political purposes." According to the bureaucrats, the only safeguard against political interference is a guarantee of structural autonomy to the department.

Two types of line bureaucrats may be less satisfied with the reform heritage, however. Lacking allies, bureaucrats in politically weak agencies may feel they have more to gain from a reorganization putting them directly under a department head. In this way they may be able to convince the department head and the chief executive of the correctness of their policy proposals and thus be more successful than they were as a more autonomous agency. And bureaucrats in agencies oriented toward policies that break sharply from the status quo may not be very enthusiastic about the merit system. They may wish to recruit persons with the same policy orientation rather than retain veteran bureaucrats who do not share their policy stance. If they can, such change-minded bureaucrats often establish a new agency and hire without using central merit system procedures.

Overhead agency bureaucrats, such as employees of the budget or finance department, personnel department, or the auditor, usually have a different orientation to fragmentation and the merit system than do line department bureaucrats. First, they have a bird's-eye view of the whole governmental framework and look with disfavor on autonomy and exceptions. Their agency culture espouses central management, and they therefore like to have all agencies under them. The mandate of the overhead agency employee, which is derived from his status as an assistant to the chief executive, is to control and coordinate the entire administration. When separate personnel systems and autonomous agencies exist, the overhead agency bureaucrats are frustrated in their mission.

While all state and urban government employees are not today in civil service systems, the majority are, and the extent of coverage is growing. This phenomenon makes it much more difficult for the legislature or chief executive to control agency personnel, since they cannot be fired without cause. Although civil service coverage is not all-inclusive, and there are ways to get around it in many cases, the bureaucracy, because of the merit system, is much more autonomous than it was fifty years ago. That line agency bureaucrats appreciate this fact is shown by their reactions to criticism of it. A recent illustration is the response of Deputy Chief Inspector Eli Lazarus to former New York City Police Commissioner Patrick Murphy's claim in January, 1972, that the civil service system restricted his power to reorganize the department: "We view any infringement of the civil service system as a return to the basic evils of patronage."[17]

STATE GOVERNMENT STRUCTURE AND PERSONNEL

A recent survey indicates that the average number of agencies per state is eighty-five which includes five agencies headed by independently elected top officials.[18] In some states, however, reorganizers have set the maximum at twenty or fewer. While two-thirds of the states have general merit systems, only a little over half of state government employees are covered, compared to over 85 percent of federal workers. Typically, it is the economically poorer states that have less comprehensive coverage, but there are exceptions. Pennsylvania, a highly developed industrial state, provides coverage for slightly more than half of its work force. In states that do not have comprehensive civil service systems, the political party organizations become personnel departments.

Interest in reorganizing fragmented state governments dates back before 1917, when Illinois consolidated its governmental structure. The principal goals of the reorganization movement have included the following:[19]

1. Concentration of authority and responsibility in the chief executive and his appointed department heads.

2. Integration of similar functions (for example, mental health and mental retardation) in the same department.

3. Replacement of multimember boards with single administrators.

4. Coordination of staff services in overhead agencies.

5. Provision for an audit (inspection of agency records to assure that programs have been implemented as mandated) by an agency independent of the executive branch.

The reorganizers, then, aspire to combine like functions and place them under a clear chain of command, with the governor at the top. In the ideal reorganization, a limit is set on the number of departments (twenty or fewer is the rule), and the governor is granted the power to supervise them through appointment, removal, management, and budget authority.

In the period 1950–1965 three-quarters of the states established study commissions to make recommendations concerning reorganization, but few of those recommendations were followed.[20] In recent years there has been an upsurge in state reorganization. One authority (see footnote 21) notes that in the period 1965–1971 twelve states underwent substantial reorganization—almost one-third of the thirty-seven states reorganized since 1937. However, reorganization in itself does not bring about centralized, coordinated policy direction and control. First, most reorganizations do not eliminate the power of key boards and commissions, but simply absorb them into the new departments, often enabling them to maintain their identity and autonomy. Breakdown of the boards usually requires legislation. Second, the governor must vigorously assert his authority, through his staff and department heads, over the new departments. Third, the governor must have adequate personal and overhead agency staff for such action, as must the department head. It is at this point that most reorganizations fail, for legislatures rarely provide enough funds for the elaborate budget and management systems necessary to the success of the reorganization. Additional staff are needed for the systems in order for the department head to evaluate all the programs for which he is responsible and to decide if and how they should be changed to achieve maximum effectiveness. It is here that the recent reorganization of Massachusetts government foundered; it is not too much to say that if the situation is not remedied, this reorganization and others like it will achieve little.

Reorganization is only an opportunity for those who wish to control agencies more tightly, not a guarantee that they can do so. As difficult as it may be to reorganize, the most difficult task of the reorganizer is to try to attain his policy goals once reorganization is a fact.[21] One scholar found "very little evidence to support the notion that executive fragmentation itself affects the content of public policy in the states," since there is no difference in spending patterns, when controlling for other variables, between more fragmented and less fragmented agencies.[22] Reorganization alone does not guarantee policy change or control

What are the policy orientations of the occupants of the top posts in the executive branch of state government? One estimate is that members of the governor's personal staff and elected executives each comprise 10 percent of the total number of state executives. Other types include political executives, policy executives, and program executives. The first of these is the gubernatorial appointee who is closely linked to the governor, and an estimated 20 to 25 percent of state executives fall in this category. The second group—policy executives—which may constitute one-third of all executives, is likely to survive change in administrations and to be more responsive to groups outside the governor's office than to the governor. The third group—program executives—may constitute one-fourth of all executives and is comprised of professionals who owe their position to their highly specialized skills.[23] Therefore, over half of state government executives have, in fact, semipermanent tenure.

Most state executives are not in civil service merit systems, but what is striking is that a substantial minority—20 percent—are indeed covered.[24] In other words, many career bureaucrats are men not only *near* the top but also *at* the top itself. Career executives are very politically conscious and are much more likely to engage in partisan activity, such as contributing money to or working for a candidate, even when it is illegal, than are comparable federal, business, or professional executives.[25] Thus, whether or not they are career civil servants, state executives are exceptionally interested in and knowledgeable about many different aspects of politics.

CITY GOVERNMENT STRUCTURE AND PERSONNEL

In this section, as well as counterpart sections throughout this book, the ways in which urban government resembles state government are not detailed so much as the features that distinguish the former from the latter are noted. Another reason the state and urban sections are not exactly parallel is lack of data; for example, there is no information available on the percentage of city executives in the political, policy, and program categories.

The typical urban governmental structure in the United States is even more fragmented than is the case with state government. The legislature and chief executive may have to share budget-making authority with a board of finance.[26] In addition, the local scene is characterized by an incredible overlap of agencies. In 1968 there were over 81,000 units of local government, only 35,000 of which were municipalities and townships (the local government forms focused on in this book). The total includes 3,000 counties; 18,000 school districts; and 21,000 other special districts.

Special districts may be responsible for such services as fire protection, water, sewers, and even mosquito control. Most special districts, as well as the other units of local government, have the power to levy taxes. Outside New England most people pay taxes both to the municipality or township and to the county, since the latter often provides services like education and police protection. For example, Blue Island, a Chicago suburb, has thirteen governmental units, ten of which levy taxes. With this kind of Balkanization, it is not surprising that there is not much coordination among local governments in the same area. Even if there were a strong desire on the part of all to cooperate to the fullest extent—which is not usually the case—the existing governmental structure makes it extremely difficult to do so. An example is the case of twelve towns near Detroit that had an obvious need to separate storm drainage from the sewer system. Although the technological remedy for the problem was readily available and the towns could easily afford it, coordination of the fourteen governmental jurisdictions within the area took ten years.[27] Attempts to consolidate these feudal arrangements into central metropolitan, or "metro," governments have resulted either in failure or in the very limited kind of metro government that exists in Miami or Nashville. In these cases metro has not supplanted local governments but has been superimposed on them, and it performs only a few metro-wide services.

Civil service coverage in cities is undoubtedly less extensive than in the fifty state governments. While one source estimates that it exists in 58 percent of cities over 25,000,[28] it is impossible to find precise figures because many civil service commissions are only nominal. For example, from data in *The Municipal Yearbook*[29] one might conclude that both New York City and Chicago have the same type of merit system, since they both have civil service commissions that perform the same functions. In fact, however, there are thousands of patronage employees in the Chicago system because of informal arrangements made to evade the law. On the other hand, there are many cities, including New York and Los Angeles, with very deeply entrenched merit systems. In New York, for example, the top merit system executives are overwhelmingly products of the ranks rather than outsiders who entered at high levels.[30]

Further, the career bureaucrat often plays a key role in cities not characterized by true merit system government. Professor Edward Banfield, an authority on politics in Chicago, frequently stresses the key role of the party organization and the comparative lack of power among career bureaucrats there; yet he reports many cases in which career bureaucrats were vital in proposing new policy measures or in implementing policy. As he notes:

> Being a civil servant is no impediment to . . . acting politically . . . .
> On the contrary, most of them are oriented not so much toward the
> impartial application of given rules . . . as toward changing the dis-

tribution of power . . . [the bureaucrats studied in this book] were extraordinarily alike in this regard. Each was quick to tell the politicians what they should and should not do. And each held—not very far out of sight—the possibility of giving trouble to any politician who acted contrary to his advice on a matter crucial to the organization.[31]

Thus, just as the presence of a civil service commission does not mean that a community inevitably has a true merit system, absence of a merit system does not mean that career bureaucrats are not present and are not extremely important. The only way to discover the nature of the actual situation in each community is to probe into the political decision-making process to evaluate the relative strength of each kind of actor.

POLICY DEVELOPMENT

Career bureaucrats have tremendous influence in policy development, as the following examples show. In the New Haven antipoverty program, "The initiative came from . . . a small group of officials within [Mayor] Lee's urban renewal bureaucracy. Acting informally and unofficially, this group established the foundations for an anti-poverty project that later would be cited nationally as a model for the country."[32]   In Atlanta, Georgia, and Raleigh, North Carolina, top-level administrators were intimately involved in policy development.[33]   Studies of Syracuse, New York, and Tucson, Arizona, found that government administrators were the principal participants in community decision making.[34]   A report on research done on the Wayne County (Detroit) Road Commission described the executive director as politically "unbeatable" in highway policy.[35]   A survey of Hawaii bureaucrats turned up evidence that they played key roles in both legislative and electoral politics.[36]   In 1969, New York City teachers were able to get the state legislature to terminate a number of educational innovations opposed by the union.[37]   An analysis of city planning politics in over 150 cities concludes that "policy-making . . . is still the prime province of the bureaucracy and the executive. . . ."[38]   This list could be extended, but it should sufficiently underscore the crucial contribution of bureaucrats to policy development.

Bureaucratic power is based primarily on three resources. The first is the bureaucrat's unrivaled expertise, or knowledge of the activities of his agency. Even outside experts from "think tanks"[39] and universities lack the specialized knowledge that the staff of an executive agency has gathered over a period of years. The second is permanency. Very few agencies die out, and individual bureaucrats are likely to outlast individual representatives of other types of actors at the state and urban levels—legislators, chief executives, and so on—with the exception of interest group representatives. Thus, the bureaucrat may lose a battle but then go on to win the war after a more ephemeral opponent shuffles off.[40]   The third resource is the prevailing respect in American society for specialized professionalism. The governmental specialist is well thought of not only for his reputed competence, but also because he contrasts favorably with those who hold office as a result of patronage. Professional bureaucrats have done their best to propagate the myth that they are neutral in policy matters and simply act, to the best of their ability, as directed by political executives.

Just as there are variations in bureaucratic culture, there are variations in bureaucratic power, the extent of which is seemingly determined by the following crucial factors.

1. *Homogeneity and intensity of bureau culture.* If bureau employees are united in adherence to bureau norms and believe strongly in them, they will be a more effective political force than if the opposite is true. This kind of unity will prevent a political executive who wants to change bureau policy from learning as much as he needs to know about the bureau, because the personnel will not do their best to enlighten him. This kind of intense support of bureau norms will enable the employees to threaten a strike or slowdown if bureau culture is threatened. In a bureau where these conditions do not hold, opponents will be able to "divide and conquer" it much more easily and will not have to worry much about the bureau as a factor in policy development.

2. *Structural autonomy.* If a bureau is well insulated structurally from the chief executive's chain of command, it will have an advantage in policy development that bureaus within that chain of command do not. State universities are usually governed by boards of trustees appointed by the governor to serve fixed, overlapping terms, and trustees cannot be removed. They choose the president and fix policy. Often, the institution may be relatively free of the state legislature's appropriations process, raising its revenue in large part through tuition and fees. This situation contrasts with that of agencies whose heads can be appointed and removed by the governor and who receive all funds from the legislature.

3. *Technical complexity of bureau activities.* The more technically complex the activities of a bureau, the more likely bureaucrats are to dominate policy development. The operation of a health or hospitals department is likely to be much less intelligible to a layman than is a department of motor vehicles. A new political executive can master within a few years the technical intricacies of the latter, but even a political executive who has an M.D. may have difficulty evaluating health care programs in areas outside his medical specialty.

4. *Size and complexity of the executive branch.* If a bureau is part of a very large executive establishment, bureaucrats are more likely to dominate policy development than if it is in a smaller executive establishment.

The larger the executive establishment, the more difficult it is for the chief executive and legislature to keep tabs on bureau operations. If the establishment is large enough, chief executive and legislative staffs are bureaucracies in their own right, eluding the control of their "masters." One reason New York City is considered ungovernable is the huge size of its government and the inability of overhead agencies to coordinate it. A city like Jackson, Mississippi, is much more manageable than New York because it is smaller; the mayor probably knows all key bureau heads personally— something the mayor of New York cannot hope to do.

5. *Political skill and aggressiveness.* Agencies differ in the extent to which they try to enlist support for their programs. Some vigorously cultivate legislators, the chief executive's staff, and interest groups; others may not work so hard. One study of two state agencies showed that one always asked for a much greater expansion of programs than the other.[41] It is difficult to determine the reasons for variations in bureau skill and aggressiveness, but they certainly exist, and one should be aware of them.

If a bureau has a homogeneous and strongly supported culture, substantial structural autonomy, highly technical functions, and political skill and aggressiveness, and is part of a large, complex executive branch, it proves to be a formidable factor in policy development. Indeed, it is no exaggeration to note that the bureau itself will probably dominate policy development. If the opposite of all these conditions is true, the bureau will be fortunate to have any weight at all in policy development.

POLICY IMPLEMENTATION

Bureaucratic power in policy implementation is greater than in policy development because the bureaucrats are the implementers. They must determine just how policy is carried out. Inevitably, they exercise discretion, since not even the wisest policy maker can forsee all the possible questions and problems that arise in carrying out a new program.

Some bureaucrats have more latitude in carrying out their assigned functions than others. Policemen, for example, have enormous discretion to decide whether to arrest someone, warn him, or simply ignore his actions. This discretion is reinforced because it is almost impossible to monitor a policeman's actions. To do so would require another policeman who would dog the first's steps. It is much easier to monitor the work of a Recreation and Parks Department maintenance worker, since one can inspect the areas he is supposed to be keeping up.

While some bureaucrats have more discretion than others, almost all bureaucrats have a substantial amount of it. Bureaucrats even write the regulations covering implementation. After a law is passed by the legislature, an order issued by the chief executive, or a decision handed down by a court, implementation falls to the agencies. Bureaucrats begin by drawing up regulations that have the force of law and that will guide them in carrying out the new policy. The regulations are usually much more detailed than the policy developed by the legislature, chief executive, or court; but some regulations can have quite an impact. Often the agency has no guidance in writing certain regulations, because the act of policy development may give no direction in a given area. For example, welfare law says clients must make their homes available for inspection by welfare workers. It does not say when, however, and welfare workers in some areas have deduced that they have the right to enter dwellings at any time without appointment. In other areas, under similar laws, this kind of visitation is not practiced. In a real sense, then, bureaucrats become legislators when they act as implementers.

In many instances even the regulations give little direction to bureaucrats. A case study of Baltimore housing inspectors exemplifies how bureaucrats can decide what a law means by the way they enforce it. Since inspectors lack the time to check all housing and the power to make landlords fix all conditions in violation of the housing code, their behavior varies with the situation. They may settle for less than minimum standards in seriously dilapidated neighborhoods; they may bargain with landlords and agree to overlook one violation if another is taken care of; and they may advise the landlords not to make repairs that are clearly his responsibility. Likewise, landlords who challenge the inspectors' authority are likely to receive the harshest possible treatment, regardless of objective conditions.[42]

Bureaucrats have ample resources to resist the orders of political executives who wish to reorient bureau policy. First, they can implement the orders directly in a solely formalistic way, not really involving themselves in a positive, aggressive, and imaginative fashion, thus negating the intent of the orders. Second, they can stymie the executive simply by immersing themselves in red tape. They can carry out orders dilatorily, and they can sometimes bring the operations of the bureau to a near halt by living in strict accordance with the rules. Most administrative agencies have a highly elaborate set of regulations that must be informally circumvented in order to accomplish anything. Thus, firemen and policemen can paralyze their departments simply by obeying all departmental rules. Third, when a political executive proposes changing bureau policy, bureaucrats may be able to design regulations giving themselves as much flexibility as possible in the new situation. They are usually asked for advice, and their expertise may lead to a code with which they feel they can live. Finally, in some cases, bureaucrats may simply refuse to obey. Edward Costikyan, former Democratic party chairman of New York County (Manhattan), related the response to an order by the mayor to proceed on a new project. One department head did nothing and was asked why. He replied, "Listen, the mayor may be for it, and he may have told you he's for it, and he may have told the press he's for it, but he hasn't told *me* he's for it."[43]

Bureaucrats, then, are often political actors of enormous importance to city and state political systems. In the following chapters their relationships with other actors are investigated.

Conclusion

There are many different types of bureaucrats, and many variations in both the goals of bureaus and the extent to which individual bureaucrats are powerful. Some key variables influencing the power of a particular bureau are its structure and culture, the technical complexity and administrative discretion involved in its work, the size of the general government of which it is a part, and the political skill of its leaders. While one can put forth tentative generalizations about bureaucratic behavior, exceptions to each generalization will be found.

CHAPTER TWO

Chief Executives

The authority vested in urban and state chief executives has increased so greatly in the twentieth century that it led one author to subtitle his study of the American governor "From Figurehead to Leader."[1] In the nineteenth century, with very few exceptions, chief executives played second fiddle to legislatures and party bosses. It was a day of dilettante chief executives; except in the very largest states and cities, the position was typically not a full-time job.[2]

This era has come to a close, but the present period is replete with problems for the chief executive who would be in fact as well as name the chief of government. And just as there are great variations in power from one bureau to another, chief executives, even when they share the same formal title, often differ greatly in policy-making power.

THE GOVERNOR: POLICY DEVELOPMENT

A general thesis of this chapter is that the governor is more important in policy development than in policy implementation. His leadership role in policy development is institutionalized in most state governments. It usually is he who presents the budget to the legislature and gives a "state of the state" message, similar to the president's State of the Union Message, complete with policy proposals. These developments, together with his veto power[3] over legislation, have made most governors the chief legislator in a very meaningful sense and, on the surface, the key policy initiator in state government. The veto power of most governors is superior to that of the president, since it usually includes an *item veto*, which enables the governor to veto not only an entire act but also individual items or sections of an act. This formal authority contributes greatly to his bargaining power with the legislature, since it usually takes a two-thirds vote of that body to override his veto. The proposals the governor sets before the legislature may be modified or rejected, but state lawmakers are unlikely to take action in policy areas where the governor has not made recommendations.

While the remarks above are accurate generalizations, there is a substantial minority of governors who do not have as much formal authority as the rest of their peers. A number of governors do not have the item veto, and one—the governor of North Carolina—has no veto at all. Fourteen governors must share preparation of the budget with a civil service appointee or a person appointed by someone else, six with several other political actors who have independent sources of strength, and the Arkansas governor with the legislature itself.

Another limitation that applies to a number of governors is the inability to run for reelection. Nine states restrict the governor to one term, and another fourteen limit tenure to two consecutive terms. While a former governor can serve again after another person has held the office, the restriction has profound implications for his role as a leader in policy development. As soon as the governor is sworn into office for a term in which he cannot succeed himself, he becomes a "lame duck." Although he may continue to exert as much influence in the first part of that term as any occupant could hope to, his last year almost inevitably means a lessening in his power, as other political actors become less interested in who the governor is than in who his successor will be. He will find it more difficult to attract new people to work for him then and to cajole reluctant officeholders, whether they be civil servants, his own appointees, or legislators, to go along with him.

The governor's power is not based solely on formal authority. A prime resource is his status as a leader of his political party. As a party leader, the governor is often the real head of his party in the legislature. In addition, he is often the leader of his party's organization, enabling him to gain the support of many groups for a policy measure. While most governors thus derive substantial power from their role in the party, some never become strong party leaders. This is most likely to happen in one-party areas, like the South, where the governor may confront legislative leaders who wish to control policy development or eventually become governor themselves. When a governor deals with a legislature controlled by the opposite party, his problems are intensified; and he is likely to encounter this difficulty since "during the 1947–68 period, there was no state that had some alternation in party control of the governorship or the legislature that completely escaped divided government."[4]

If a governor has substantial formal authority, a party leadership role, and personal political skill, he can be considered a strong governor. As such, he is almost certainly a key figure in policy development. Such a strong governor can expand state programs, as New York's Rockefeller did in the 1960s, or curb them, as California's Reagan did in the same period.[5] A weak governor, lacking these resources, is unable to point to such achievements. Yet, whether a governor is strong or weak, he is dependent in a very real sense on the bureaucracy in developing policy. Most of the items in both the legislative program and the budget submitted by a governor originate in the bureaucracy.

A governor depends on the bureaucracy for program advice and indeed *expects* the agencies to come up with proposals for new programs. Assume that he is interested in the treatment of drug addiction. He has several options open to him: he can appoint a special study commission, hire a professional consultant, or obtain information from state agencies concerned with the problem. The commission and the consultant are likely to gather much information from the state agencies themselves, but if they ignore those agencies, they must go to other government agencies to learn about drug addiction. Even a governor determined to by-pass his own bureaucrats in policy development eventually becomes dependent to a great extent upon bureaucrats in some other governmental jurisdiction. In most cases a governor is unlikely to rely on a study commission and consultants for policy development advice; he is more likely to look to bureaucrats in his own agencies.

A governor's dependence upon bureaucrats varies among policy areas. The more technically complex the work of a bureau and the more structurally autonomous it is, the less impact he has on its policy development. For example, health is one program area where a governor is utterly dependent upon the advice of experts, because of its involved technical nature. Of course, he can accept or reject the advice, but in any event he is unlikely to be able to evaluate it. On the other hand, a governor is less likely to rely on the advice of bureaucrats when he makes a decision about a new basic tax or a large increase in an existing one. He is more likely to talk to party leaders and consult opinion polls to determine which option will be least unpopular with the voters. But even here, his decision may be greatly influenced by revenue estimates for each tax made by bureaucrats in his tax department or budget office.

To be sure, strong and weak governors vary in their dependence upon the bureaucracy. A strong governor is likely to have more adequate personal and institutional staff resources with which to evaluate bureaucratic advice than is a weak governor. For example, in his budget office a strong governor may well have analysts whose full-time job is to evaluate bureau performance, and who have thus built up a store of expertise in certain subject areas. These overhead agency bureaucrats are likely to be sympathetic to the governor since they share his broad policy perspective, rather than the narrower outlook of the line agency. A strong governor's personal staff, who are not career bureaucrats, may also include some advisers who are knowledgeable about policies in specific areas, although such persons constitute only a small minority.[6] A weak governor is unlikely to have any substantial control of overhead agencies or to have a personal staff with any subject-matter specialists.

Whether a governor is strong or weak, it often seems that the most he can do to be independent of the bureaucracy in policy development is to decide on which individual bureaucrats he should rely. He or his appointed department heads look within line agencies for advisers and then may promote them to higher positions. But he must rely on *some* bureaucrat for information because persons outside the bureaucracy do not have the requisite detailed knowledge.

The editors of a recent major work on governors argue that the governor has become "the prime mover of significant politics and administration at the state level . . ." and that there are few program areas in which he is not a leader.[7] We would not argue with the thesis that the governor is a leader, but the prime mover is the bureaucracy itself.

THE GOVERNOR: POLICY IMPLEMENTATION

Constitutional provisions relating to control of the administrative branch of state government divide power between the chief executive and the legislature. For this reason, no matter what other ideal conditions may exist in his favor, the governor is going to find himself frustrated at times in his attempt to oversee, coordinate, and manage the administrative apparatus of which he is nominally the chief. While marked variations in the power of policy implementation exist, all governors are often crossed in the attempt to impose their wills on their administrative subordinates. Often these restrictions are imbedded in the state constitution, which is much more difficult to amend than it is to change laws passed by the legislature. Five types of limitations seem particularly relevant to the governor's policy implementation power.[8]

First, the governor must usually share power with independently elected executive officials. For example, in 1969 forty-two states had elected attorneys general; forty-one, treasurers; thirty-nine, secretaries of state; twenty-nine, auditors; and twenty-three, superintendents of education. When the electorate elects a ticket split between candidates of both major parties, the governor has a very difficult time influencing officeholders of the opposition party. In Massachusetts, for example, a recent pattern has been for a new Republican governor to find that all other elected executive officials are Democratic. A Republican treasurer in Wisconsin recently refused to honor the salary voucher of a state commission member appointed by the Democratic governor.[9] Even in cases where the other elected officials may be of the same party as the governor, he may have problems controlling them or influencing them, especially if they are ambitious politicians who covet his job and who owe him nothing for their election. If a governor is a strong party leader whose party sweeps all the top state offices, however, he may be able to overcome the problem of the unresponsive elected executive. He can do so by making sure that the party nominates individuals responsive to him. And, of course, there are variations in the numbers of elected executives per state, so that some governors find this problem negligible or less irksome than others.

Second, the governor's power to appoint persons to and remove them from administrative positions is often restricted. As noted in Chapter 1, legislatures seem to enjoy creating boards, commissions, and other executive agencies to which the governor cannot name members. In some cases appointees serve a fixed term, and only when a term expires can the governor nominate successors. In other cases he has no authority whatsoever to appoint members; it lies with the legislature or other boards or commissions. Even when the governor can name persons to office, he usually has to gain legislative approval for them. One researcher has calculated that the governors in only thirteen states name as many as half the appointees to the key departments. In fact, the highest rating of any governor in this evaluation was that for the governor of Tennessee, who has the authority to name 73 percent of the heads of sixteen key governmental functions.[10]

Besides the problem of limited authority, the governor may also often find it difficult to attract persons whom he desires to serve in state government, largely because salaries, set by the legislators, are not as high as comparable positions in industry. An example is that of Governor Thomas Meskill of Connecticut, elected in 1970. Governor Meskill made it known that his prime criterion for appointment to key executive positions was personal loyalty to himslef. However, he retained fully one-fifth of the political executives, commissioners, and deputy commissioners who had served under his Democratic predecessor. This group of executives, who had spent careers as either professionals or bureaucrats, were presumably kept on because Meskill could not have easily attracted persons with the necessary expertise.

Equally important as the statutory and constitutional constraints on appointment is the power of other actors. Party organization leaders and interest group representatives often sponsor individuals for key executive appointments, and the governor may feel that he has no choice but to accept their recommendations, given their past support and/or their influence in the legislature. The governor is in an even worse position insofar as his power to remove appointed officials is concerned. Many gubernatorial appointees serve fixed terms. To remove appointees who do not serve fixed terms, the governor may need legislative consent. He usually has to "show cause" and may have to invoke a public hearing. Under the circumstances, one can understand why he may tolerate troublesome or incompetent subordinates rather than attempt to remove them. Some governors find the appointee-removal problem less troublesome than do others. The governor of Tennessee is less hampered by it than the governor of Arizona, who can name only 17 percent of his top appointees. But no governor is entirely free of this limitation.

Third, the governor's authority to manage through budgetary controls may be restricted. The limitations on the governor's budget preparation authority in a number of states have already been noted; but the budgetary process does not end with the passage of an appropriations act, since the monies appropriated do not automatically go to the bureaus, but must be allotted to them by the central budget office. This office may allot less than was appropriated. It may also allot funds at a variable rate. Funds are usually allotted on a quarterly basis and in the same proportion per quarter, but a central agency may be able to allot funds at a rate of 10 percent one quarter, 30 percent the next, and so on. One scholar argues that the budget or finance director "is often the second most powerful official in local or state government, and recent trends would seem to buttress his position."[11] Most governors enjoy substantial authority in this area, but a large minority are handicapped. Such controls can be of great importance in influencing bureau behavior, and if a governor lacks them, he lacks an important resource for policy implementation.

Fourth, the authority of the governor and his key political executives to control agency personnel is circumscribed. Civil service systems limit the chief executive by establishing criteria for entry, promotion, job classi- fication, and removal. Where a civil service system does not exist, and this is the case in many areas of state government, the governor and his key subordinates have wide discretion over personnel matters.

Finally, most governors have limited reorganization powers. The presi- dent of the United States has the authority to submit a plan for reorganiza- tion of executive departments to Congress. If neither house of Congress moves within sixty days to veto his proposal, it becomes law. Only ten of fifty governors, however, enjoy even this limited authority to reorganize their own administrations. Instead, most of them have to go hat-in-hand to the legislature to ask for such a grant because they have no legal basis to take the initiative in reorganization. Reorganization can be a crucial man- agement tool, ending structural autonomy and establishing bureaus directly within the governor's chain of command.

Several surveys of gubernatorial policy-making power underscore the importance of the factors just examined. One study, which polled in- cumbent governors on the powers they lacked that could aid them signifi- cantly in effecting their programs, elicited responses indicating that they were greatly frustrated by the absence of appointive powers.[12] Another survey, based on reports from fourteen political scientists who spent brief periods on gubernatorial staffs, led the author to conclude that whatever problems the governor might have in influencing the state legislature, he was more successful with it than with administrators.[13] Another scholar found that "in states where governors have stronger formal powers adminis- trators acknowledge somewhat greater control by governors than in states where governors are weaker."[14] Not to be forgotten are the variations in gubernatorial authority over policy implementation. The governor of New York is very much a chief administrator; the governor of Florida is perhaps slightly more of a chief administrator than several other state officials.

Another factor that has bearing not only on policy development but also on policy implementation is the governor's strength as a party or legislative leader. As a leading student of the governor's office said twenty years ago in remarks still valid today:

What is less obvious but nonetheless of crucial importance to the governor in his management role is that the power base which the governor establishes in the legislature is a fact which conditions the whole relationship between the governor and his department heads. A typical situation in most states is that the governor is dealing with many department heads who are independent of his control so far as appointment and removal is concerned. In the case of a disagreement between the governor and the head of such a department, the governor's most potent weapon is a threat to reduce the department's appropriations through a reduction of its part of the executive budget. This reduction will stick only if the governor is in a very strong position vis-à-vis the legislature. When the governor is not in a strong legislative position, the department head knows that he can secure reinstatement of the reduced item and, consequently, he can flout the governor's authority with impunity. . . . There are such potent organizations as the agricultural extension services, the bureaus of fish and game, the preserve of the state's sportsmen, and other agencies varying from state to state which represent potent political power which even a strong governor must treat with respect. The governor with weak legislative support is virtually helpless in enforcing his administrative edicts, save in those departments which he can control by appointment. Even here he is likely to be stuck with his original appointees, since in many states the governor's removal power does not extend even to the officers whom he appoints. This particular aspect of the interrelation between the governor's role in management and his role in legislation is sometimes overlooked, but it is of great significance in practical administration.[15]

One scholar argues that Southern governors have achieved such ascendancy over the legislature that they need not fear any legislative interference in administrative matters. This dominance is based on the governor's control of jobs, contracts, highway funds, and capital improvement funds. Checks on the governor come less from the legislature than from an increasingly professionalized bureaucracy.[16]

The most important recent study of the governor argues that the governor has become much more of an administrative coordinating force in state government in the postwar period.[17] A number of changes have concentrated more effective means of management in the governor's hands. Over two-thirds of the states have established departments of administration in recent years. Within many of these departments are management analysts whose task is to devise bureau organization to make program delivery both more effective and more responsive to the governor. State budget offices increasingly stress new types of budgetary systems designed to promote the same goals.[18] Central planning has received greater emphasis and, like the management and budget tools, is coming more and more under the authority of the governor. While governors have thus increased their policy implementation resources, the limitations on their powers of implementation seem more striking than any recent gains. Certainly the *potential* administrative power of governors has increased, but their capacity to avail themselves of these resources has not.

The most important reason for this imbalance lies in the governor's own view of the relative importance of his different responsibilities. The role of chief administrator is only one of the governor's responsibilities, and it is usually viewed by him as one of his least important roles. The governor is usually his party's head, the chief legislator, and a leading symbol of government. Further, many governors have ambitions to go on to the Senate or the White House and may thus view administrative responsibilities as a hindrance to successful prosecution of the campaign to ascend to higher office by establishing a reputation as a policy initiator.

As Coleman Ransone wrote twenty years ago, "It is particularly interesting to note that administrative problems as presented by department heads and officials of state agencies and institutions counted for only ten percent of the total number of callers received by the governor. . . . The average governor spends relatively little time on the conferences with his department heads on administrative problems."[20] A more recent study of Governor Richard Ogilvie of Illinois shows that he spent 27 percent of his time in June 1971 on public relations, 11 percent on political leadership, and 19 percent on management of state government.[21] Governors continue, then, to devote only a portion of their time to policy implementation.

None of this is surprising when one considers the reasons a governor is nominated or elected. The most important factors here are a facility for electoral politics. Among prime resources for an elective politician are extroverted affability, a gift for small talk, a memory for faces and names, experience and skill in dealing with party organization leaders, an appealing face, public speaking ability, a pleasant television manner, and the capacity to manage his campaign or to delegate its management to skilled operators. Only the last of these has any relationship to the management of large bureaucratic organizations, and this relationship is tenuous. Management skill is unrelated to electoral success, so it is no surprise that few governors come to office with such a skill.

One study notes that a high percentage of a governor's personal staff is recruited from his campaign staff or from other areas unrelated to administration.[22] This is significant because such individuals are unlikely to have had much experience working in and understanding large bureaucratic organizations; they must spend a great deal of time on the job, learning basic facts about the nature and control of state agencies. Another study shows conclusively that the governor himself almost always lacks substantial administrative background, just as every president since Franklin Roosevelt has been without significant managerial experience before his election.[23] The consequences of this deficiency mean that, typically, when chief executives try to control "their" bureaucracy, they simply take restrictive measures, such as cutting budgets and refusing to fill positions that have been vacated. This is a far cry, however, from the evaluation of government programs to see which make the most sense in terms of costs and benefits, and of truly understanding the nature of state government programs. Although there are exceptions to this norm, such as Rockefeller of New York, they are few and far between. Most governors do not use their overhead agencies to conduct management analysis studies to be used as a basis for administrative changes.

The future may bring significant changes. The means for increased gubernatorial management are increasingly available; and a governor who is relatively unencumbered with formal restrictions, is a strong party and legislative leader, and *wants* to be a strong chief administrator can be.

CITY CHIEF EXECUTIVE: POLICY DEVELOPMENT

The Mayor

Compared to governors, mayors lack formal authority and are thus handicapped in their policy development role. Half of all mayors lack veto power of any kind; half are elected to two-year terms of office; and almost half of all cities elect other executive officials.[24] A survey of cities over 50,000 found that only 39 of 151 mayor-council governments has a strong mayor form.[25]

As in the case of the governor, formal authority is a key determinant in making a mayor strong or weak. One study of Detroit, a strong-mayor city, notes that although a number of boards and commissions exist, the mayor's appointment and removal powers make him a leader. Specifically, the study described a policy shift in urban renewal away from public housing to private redevelopment as the result of the election of a new mayor.[26]

Although these formal restrictions make the job of mayor arduous, a skilled political operative and party leader can use limited resources to become a major figure in policy development. The record of Richard Lee of New Haven, Connecticut, exemplifies this point. Mayor from 1953 to 1969, Lee was able to launch and implement the most comprehensive urban renewal program in any American city. He did so principally through the resources available to him as chief of his party, and by his skill at persuasion and negotiation with the federal government and groups within the community.[27]

Likewise, Jeffrey Pressman's study of mayoral leadership in Oakland, California, a manager-council community, indicates that the extent to which the mayor is able to exercise power in policy development depends largely on his personality and willingness to exploit his meager resources. Pressman points out that a great deal of the mayor's influence is based on his prestige and legitimacy, which he can use to prevail upon different groups to go along with him on certain issues. Further, the mayor is the presiding officer at city council meetings and appoints council committees, which gives him an opportunity to affect discussions and outcomes. The mayor of Oakland cultivated one councilman whose chief interest lay in an airport–golf course by creating a golf course committee and making the councilman its chairman and only member. Informal cultivation of council-men at social occasions may also pay very good dividends. Another re-source that even a weak mayor may enjoy is the authority to name mem-bers to many city commissions; this can be valuable if he is in office long enough to make a number of appointments.[28] Thus, it is possible for a mayor to exert leadership even in extremely difficult circumstances. A strong mayor plays an even more important role in policy development, but only if he is politically skilled. No more than the presidency or the governorship is the mayoralty a proper place for a politically unskilled actor.

Duane Lockard distinguishes four styles of mayoral leadership that are useful to consider in surveying the urban scene. The *reformer* comes to office after waging a crusade against evils perpetrated by "bosses." Re-formers may differ in their political ideology and solutions to problems, but they share a moralistic fervor, at least in their rhetoric. They are typically blue-blooded WASPs (Philadelphia's Joseph Clark and Richardson Dilworth of the 1950s; New York's John Lindsay), although Fiorello La Guardia, mayor of New York from 1934 to 1945, must be numbered in their ranks.

The *program politician* is a tough-minded activist determined to change the city. This type of mayor is the number one "booster" of the com-munity, whether his program is urban renewal or the construction of a city arena. Some recent examples of this type are New Haven's Richard Lee, Providence's Joseph Doorley, Indianapolis's Richard Lugar, and Cleve-land's Carl Stokes.

Lockard's two other types are the *evader*, who seeks to avoid contro-versy, and the *stooge*, front man for a machine;[29] but they are not so much in evidence now as during the heyday of the political machines. Perhaps another type would be the *mediator*,[30] who is less concerned with policy leadership than arbitration of conflicts. The mediator differs from the evader in deliberately seeking to intervene and mediate disputes among other actors when the occasion arises, rather than retreating from the scene. Chicago's Richard Daley and former New York Mayor Robert Wagner illustrate this category.

The reformer and program politician are likely to be greatly concerned with the bureaucracy, since they wish to change city government programs. They will be much more likely to try to "shake up" city agencies through the introduction of new evaluation and budget systems, reorganization of agency structure, and the appointment of like-minded persons as depart-ment heads and bureau chiefs. The evader, stooge, and mediator are likely to be concerned with such matters only if a crisis erupts, and will most likely fail to follow up on supervision of the bureaucracy when the crisis dies down.

What is the policy development role of mayors in council-manager cities? Research on council-manager cities of over 100,000 population indicates there is a great deal of variation. Of the forty-five mayors surveyed, thirty had influence in setting the council's agenda, and thrity-seven in making recommendations to the council, although they had no formal authority to do so.[31] Another study found that popular election of the mayor (as opposed to alternative modes such as selecting as mayor the councilman with the largest number of votes) was associated with greater mayoral participation in the budget-making process. The mayor does not gain any more formal authority through independent election, but apparently he is more likely to be a leader when chosen in this manner.[32] To summarize, as Pressman concludes about Oakland, "The mayor does have certain political resources . . . and an adept political man can pyramid those resources. . . . A mayor's lot is not a happy one, but it is not a hopeless one, either."[33]

The City Manager

The city manager is a professional appointed by the city council to be the chief executive for the municipality. The council can remove him at any time by majority vote. The manager has full legal authority over administrative matters, whether they relate to the personnel system, budgeting, or other aspect. He has no formal voting or veto powers. Usually, there is also a mayor in the community, but in terms of formal authority, he occupies what is largely a secondary and ceremonial role.

The city manager is as likely to be a leader in policy development as is the mayor, although there are important differences in style and resources. The manager has no right of tenure. The mayor, of course, is elected and serves a fixed term. On the other hand, the manager ordinarily has a much better understanding of the nature of urban administration and much greater expertise in urban management. But he may be handicapped compared to the mayor, who is likely to be a local person and to know the politics of the city like the palm of his hand. The manager is a bird of passage who moves from one city to another, as do other professionals. Finally, both the mayor and the manager enjoy certain kinds of legitimacy, though from quite different sources. The mayor is perceived as a legitimate figure because he is an elected official. The manager, in contrast, gains legitimacy from his expertise in management.

Although these major differences distinguish the mayor from the manager, the successful manager is as likely to be a key policy maker as is the successful mayor. In other words, the policy-administration dichotomy does not hold water, a fact acknowledged by the International City Management Association in 1952 when it revised its code of ethics to read: "The city manager as a community leader submits policy proposals to the council and provides the council with facts and advice on matters of policy to give the council a basis for making decisions on community goals." The term "leader" is a euphemism; the manager is a politician.[34] He is a politician because he is concerned not only with administrative detail but also with policy making, both in the development of new policies and in the implementation of policy. Anyone who doubts this has only to look at the major empirical studies of the manager. A survey of 140 managers in towns of 2,500–10,000 population found that 83 percent felt that a city manager should play a leading role in policy making in his community. The survey concludes that "in sum, whether they discussed their role in a theoretical, general, or specific way, managers emerge as policy leaders in all three types of cities."[35] A study of fifty-eight managers in the San Francisco region made the same point: "In city legislative politics, city managers participate as policy executives. . . . There is no reluctance to admit to activities that establish their intimate involvement in the policy process."[36] An analysis of North Carolina managers led to the same conclusion: "Managers participate actively in the process . . . most mayors and councilmen encourage the manager to initiate action which may result in a policy decision."[37]

What resources does the manager possess that explain his key place in policy development? First, his functional task in government is to provide and evaluate policy alternatives for the council. He is usually prepared, and often expected, to make a policy recommendation. Second, the manager's resources explain why, in Pressman's phrase, "there is a strong tendency . . . for administration to devour politics."[38] Pressman notes that in Oakland the mayor is paid $7,500 and councilmen $4,600—and thus find it financially difficult to work full time, while the manager's $40,000 salary enables him to do so. In addition, the manager usually has far greater staff resources, including not only personal assistants but, potentially, all city employees. Thus, he has much more information about city government than any other actor.

Like other actors, managers vary in the extent to which they are leading policy developers. One scholar has found that the manager devotes most of his time to administration and obtains more satisfaction from it than from other jobs.[39] Another found a great range in the behavior of managers regarding controversial and innovative policies:

> The commitment and scope of [city managers'] policy activities differ noticeably on major issues of innovation and leadership. Managers range from those who resemble political chief executives to others who limit their nonroutine policy activity to informing and advising the council. The point to make is that while all city managers involve themselves in the policy process, their policy style can differ markedly on controversial matters.[40]

Then again, one can say the same thing about mayors.

CITY CHIEF EXECUTIVE: POLICY IMPLEMENTATION

The Mayor

The local chief executive, whether he is mayor or manager, confronts the same kinds of frustrations as the governor in trying to manage a bureaucracy. If the mayor is strong in formal authority, he can be a formidable figure in policy implementation, because he has substantial power to create or abolish positions, to make temporary transfers, to administer a contingency fund, to appoint and remove officials, and to administer budget funds. If a mayor is a strong party leader, he may be able to circumvent fragmented authority by skillfully utilizing his party role, as Mayor Daley of Chicago and former Mayor Richard Lee of New Haven have done. For example, Lee gained effective control of the New Haven boards of aldermen, zoning appeals, and finance through his control of the nominating machinery and use of patronage. Nineteen of thirty-three aldermen were economically vulnerable to mayoral attack (eleven were city employees, three had close relatives who worked for the city, and five did business with the city). Several Board of Finance members did business with the city and could thus be influenced by the mayor.[41]

The mayor's role as chief administrator, however, is still characterized by frequent bargaining with opponents and would-be allies rather than the imposition of ukases from above. Studies of New Haven politics under Lee and Chicago politics under Daley indicate that this is indeed the case.[42] Further, no mayor can be a leader in every or even most areas of his city government. Another study of New Haven notes that although Lee was nationally recognized as an exceptionally strong mayor, "in the more traditional areas of city administration [education, police, health], Lee's status never matched his status in urban renewal."[43] (For "more traditional" substitute "more professionalized and more structurally autonomous" to have a better idea why these agencies remained more powerful than others.) Another factor that has arisen to bedevil both the mayor and the manager is the new militancy of public unions. By demanding a voice in both work conditions and departmental policy, unions have lessened the impact of city chief executives on policy implementation.

The chief executive has more control over the bureaucracy than any other single actor. A survey of the mayors of manager-council cities indicates that even the weak chief executive can wield substantial weight in policy implementation, influencing the selection of department heads, city board and committee members, and citizen advisory board members. As the authors conclude, "The mayor does operate in the bureaucratic arena in one-quarter to one-third of the cities surveyed."[44] While this may be true, mayors, like governors, come to the job without experience in management, placing them at a disadvantage vis-à-vis the bureaucracy.

The City Manager

Most managers enjoy an edge over the other chief executives in state and city government in policy implementation. The typical city charter grants the manager sole authority to play a role in administrative matters, giving him authority equal or superior to that of the strong mayor. Equally important is the manager's training and experience in administrative management, and this administrative primacy may have far-reaching consequences. As Pressman comments in his Oakland study:

> The city manager defines "policy" and "administration" in such a way that "administration" turns out to be very large and "policy" is very small. When Mayor Reading complained in July 1968 that the police chief's stringent restrictions on policemen's use of guns . . . constituted a dangerous policy decision which should be overturned by the council, the city manager disagreed. The manager's reasoning was clear: "A policy decision would be that policemen in Oakland should carry guns. Administrative decisions should be when they should carry guns, where they should carry guns, and how they should use those guns."[45]

There are, however, some manager-council governments where the manager is greatly restricted in authority and where incumbent managers have no substantial previous experience in administration.[46] And, of course, managers, like other chief executives, vary in personal skill.

Most managers eclipse the mayor and the council in the politics of policy implementation. The former, in particular, may intervene, but he remains secondary to the manager, thanks to the manager's expertise, full-time job status, and staff resources. Compared to the strong mayor, the manager has the advantage as policy implementer, since he does not have to be concerned with reelection or, unless he wishes, with policy development in innovative and controversial areas.

Like all other chief executives, the manager cannot dominate his own bureaucrats. He may wield greater influence over them than most mayors or governors do over their bureaucrats, but he is ultimately dependent upon them in the same way as other chief executives.

Conclusion

The chief executive may often be more of a figurehead than a chief administrator. To be chief administrator, the chief executive needs substantial grants of formal authority, strong overhead agencies, party and legislative support, sophistication in management techniques, political skill, and the will to be chief administrator. Although some chief executives have all these resources, most do not. To the extent that they lack any or all of these resources, chief executives are handicapped in managing the bureaucracy.

CHAPTER THREE

Legislatures and Courts

LEGISLATURES

Legislatures have not kept pace with other branches of government in the twentieth century. Whether one examines the different levels of government in the United States or scrutinizes the governments of foreign countries, most authorities agree that legislatures play a less independent policy-making role than was formerly the case. This decline is found at both the development and implementation stages of policy making.

Legislatures at all levels of American government play a smaller part in policy making today than they did at the turn of the century, when they faced a chief executive who did not have nearly the authority of his contemporary counterpart,[1] and a much smaller, less professional bureaucracy. In the much simpler society of the nineteenth century, it was relatively easy for legislators to be aware both of what government agencies were doing and of major social developments. Today there is just too much going on for legislators to keep well informed, unless they develop elaborate information-gathering and evaluation structures. This is precisely what most legislatures at the urban and state levels have not done, so they have inevitably become dependent upon the bureaucracy. Some legislatures have kept pace, and others show signs that they adapt to changing circumstances, but most operate very much as they did at the turn of the century.

Most legislatures are characterized by low pay for members, sessions of limited duration, and lack of clerical and professional staff. As a result, most legislative jobs are part-time in nature. There is a great deal of turnover among legislators from one session to the next; many eschew running for reelection because they cannot afford the costs in money or time incurred in holding a second job. Legislators must confront bureaucrats and chief executives who are full-time officials with far superior information-gathering and policy-control resources. No wonder, then, that governors and big-city mayors are today regarded as the "chief legislators" of their governments.[2]

In addition, legislators who would be policy makers are bedeviled even more than chief executives by the demands exacted by other roles. As representatives they must often act as "errand boys," providing service in response to constituent requests, whether these be for intercession on a state contract award, provision of a patronage job, or the grant of an exception to city health regulations.[3] If they are interested in reelection, legislators will spend as much time as chief executives do in "fence mending," appearing at countless public functions in their districts.

A number of legislatures have recently demonstrated that they can become important policy makers. The difference between strong and weak bodies is due principally to the perception legislators have of their own role, for they have the law-making authority to end most of the formal restrictions on themselves. But if legislators are content to take a back seat to other actors, and bask in the prestige and formal ceremonial aspects of their office, run errands for constituents, or concern themselves principally with patronage matters, they will not be key policy makers.

STATE LEGISLATURES

Policy Development

In the analysis of legislative power, it is necessary to distinguish among different manifestations of the legislature. The first is the legislature as a whole, which acts primarily in formal votes on the floor of the legislature. The second is the legislative party system; the two parties deliberate in caucus throughout the session to lay out their views on policy matters. The third is legislative standing committees, which have separate responsibilities, such as education, welfare, and appropriations. The fourth is the individual legislator of more than average power, whether party or committee leader. Because legislatures are large multimember bodies, the strength of each component can vary. One legislature may be weak as an overall policy developer, while some of its individual committees and members may be very powerful in specialized areas. In other legislatures the party leaders may be forceful, and all the committees weak. In this book the characterization of legislatures as weak or strong refers to their overall performance. A legislature that does not assert itself as a policy developer on the floor, or through its party leaders or committees, is a weak institution, whether or not it has a few strong committees or members.

Although state legislatures have taken a number of steps to improve their effectiveness in recent years, a leading study published in 1971 still refers to them as "sometime governments."[4] At that point in time, fourteen of the fifty met biennially, and many others were in session each year for no more than a few months; many constitutions restricted the legislature in such basic areas as taxing and spending;[5] and legislators were paid an average annual salary of $6,600 and typically had little or no professional staff assistance.[6] Thus, the average legislator was a part-time lawmaker who lacked the support necessary to do a very effective job in creating proposals for policy development. Turnover among legislators is very high; one study found that 76 percent of committee chairmen in the Alabama senate, 50 percent in the Maryland and Kentucky senates, and 43 percent in the Georgia senate had served only one term as legislators.[7]

With this lack of experience, chairmen are greatly handicapped in coming to grips with the functions of state government.

It is for these reasons that the Citizens Conference on State Legislatures was founded in 1965, with the goal of transforming "state legislatures into twentieth-century institutions of government."[8] The conference is a descendant of other reform groups that have tried to improve the functioning of various forms or branches of government. That such a group came into existence and remains highly active is ample testimony to the failure of state legislatures to keep pace with change.

Most legislatures seem to define their policy development role as one of review, modification, and veto. They themselves usually do not formulate drafts of laws, but modify those originating elsewhere. Of course, even the most inept legislature can wield substantial power by turning down proposals made by others. But here the legislature has handicapped itself in policy development and can only lash out without any grasp of the programs or issues involved.

While legislators usually have a good understanding of issues directly affecting them and their constituents, they are handicapped in other areas of less direct impact by their lack of time, staff, and expertise. The more technically complex an issue, the more handicapped is the legislature. And since more and more key issues involve advanced technology, whether they be questions of pollution abatement or medical care, those legislatures that do not modernize are increasingly handicapped.

As far back as 1942, two scholars discovered that most laws enacted by the New York state legislature originated in administrative agencies—federal, state, or local. Of 884 laws passed that year, 502 came from agencies; only 119 from the legislature; and the balance from interest groups, government employee associations, and the judiciary. Further, the study concluded that the legislation sponsored by administrative agencies was certainly no less important than that from other government sources and that it was more important than legislation from nongovernment sources.[9] Thus, the New York state legislature, which has long been one of the most modern and best staffed, was not an initiator. While there is great power in being able to modify or veto policies, another facet of power-policy initiation seems to evade most state legislatures.

The record of those few states that have "modernized" their legislatures shows that the legislature can be a very different kind of political actor from what is generally the case. The California legislature is widely regarded as the most effective because it meets in open-ended annual sessions; it has a large excellent staff; and its members were paid an annual salary of $19,200 in 1972, the highest in the nation. These resources have enabled California to innovate in areas undreamed of by most state legislatures, among which are automobile pollution control, mental retardation programs, and minority-group employment.[10] And California is not alone;

legislatures in New York, Illinois, Florida, and other states also boast impressive resources with which to develop their own policy alternatives.[11] Illinois Republicans in the legislature, for example, now set forth their own program statement, regardless of which party controls the governor's chair. However, to repeat, at the present time the performance of most state legislatures does not resemble that of California's. The questions of how, when, and why some legislatures decide to become policy makers and why others retain the status quo most be resolved by future research.

Policy Implementation

Since most state legislatures are in neither plenary nor committee session most of the year, and since they lack adequate staff, there is simply not very much they can do to oversee the activities of administrative agencies on a comprehensive basis. In Virginia, for example, the legislature now convenes annually; this means that it meets for sixty days in even-numbered years, and for thirty days in odd-numbered years.[12] Thus, unless it is called into special session, it does not work as a body almost 90 percent of the time.

Although most legislatures do not have as short a session as Virginia's, none of them is permanently in session. And while it is not necessary for the legislature as a whole to be in session to exercise administrative oversight, it is necessary for legislative committees to be able to meet. They do not do so in Virginia, or in another twenty-five states.[13] Further, in a number of states where this kind of permanent committee structure exists, it is not used by legislators.

A 1961 report, which is somewhat dated but not radically so, notes that only twelve state legislatures carried out continuing, simultaneous studies of revenue and spending, budget review and analysis, and post-auditing.[14] At the federal level, post-auditing, or a careful scrutiny of the records of agencies to be sure that their policies and expenditures were consonant with the legislature's desires, is performed by the General Accounting Office (GAO), an agency responsible to Congress. The GAO inspects an agency's accounts to see that funds allocated for a certain program are spent only on that program. In 1969 twenty-seven state legislatures had no such relationship to the post-audit function; in nineteen states, the legislature chose the official in charge of auditing; and in four other states, it shared this power with an executive agency. In seventeen of the twenty-seven states in which the legislature did not share in the post-audit function, the auditing official (identified variously in the different states) was a constitutionally designated elective executive.[15] Although there is some movement toward legislative assumption of the audit, for the legislature to assume fully the post-audit function, it would require in many states that the constitution be amended—a very difficult task.

A legislature that wants to play a key part in policy implementation can do so. The substantial legislative role in administration has already been noted: the legislature creates the structure of the executive branch, has the power of the purse, and determines the type of personnel system, and how and by whom key executives are appointed.[16] A survey of state government executives indicates that more agency heads than not feel the legislature has greater control over their agency than does the governor.[17] State legislatures which want to play a key role in policy implementation can do so. An example of a legislature that plays a key role in policy implementation is New York state's, whose Legislative Commission on Expenditure Review examines the execution of state programs in detail. Recently it has produced lengthy program audit reports probing areas such as manpower training, narcotics control, public housing, and fishing and wildlife research, making recommendations to the legislature about ways in which these programs should be changed. If and when state legislatures decide to play a more assertive role in policy making, they can do so. At present, they choose not to.

CITY LEGISLATURES

Policy Development

The city council is an even more part-time, poorly paid, poorly staffed, and constitutionally restricted form of government than is the state legislature. Its authority is likely to stem from a charter granted by the state legislature and thus cannot be expanded by the council itself. The council typically meets at night, when councillors are free from their full-time nongovernmental jobs. Levenson's survey of Connecticut councillors found that one-quarter of them complained about the way their elective office robbed them of time and money.[18] Even where councillors have full-time, adequately salaried jobs, the mayor or manager is likely to be the chief legislator.[19] Indeed, the research literature on council-manager government, the form in which the council alone is supposed to make policy, is a litany to councilmanic insignificance:

> Members of the council did not emerge as either general policy innovators or as general policy leaders. . . . In both policy innovation and leadership, the role of the councilman was a relatively modest one. . . .[20]

> Managers generally deplore the lack of policy initiation by councilmen. . . . In the sample cities examined in this study it appears that most councilmen are either unwilling or unable to play a major leadership role in policy initiation. . . . Councilmen, to overstate the case, are men without a role in policy-making. . . . They can be said to make policy only in the sense that they must vote for or against measures.[21]

Almost every study that has examined the policy behavior of the city manager agrees [that] . . . most city councils fail to exercise much political leadership. . . .[22]

What about mayor-council government? A survey of Los Angeles concludes that "the career level of administration is active in all phases of statute lawmaking. It dominates the initiating, synthesizing, and legislative manipulation phases of bill enactment."[23] This finding is especially noteworthy because the Los Angeles council is part of a weak-mayor system and might be expected to be more assertive than usual in that setting. One writer, in fact, refers to this full-time council as "very powerful."[24] As in New York State, bureaucrats are the "chief legislator." In Boston, a strong-mayor city, "few councilmen have the time, interest, or ability to suggest policy innovations or to criticize in a serious way the policies of the administration." One Boston councilman related the story of his request to the police commissioner to outline his program for the year ahead, only to have the commissioner refuse to do so.[25]

As is true of the state legislature, however, the city legislature that wishes to be more assertive can be, as a study of four Wisconsin cities indicates:

In Beta and Gamma, the manager was a key leadership figure and a policy innovator. In Alpha he had a vigorous council, which itself sought to lead, and which shared policy making with him. In fact, his role as a leader was preserved there mostly by the deliberate intent of a council that was strongly committed to the principle of professional administration. In Delta, the council would not permit the manager to serve as either leader or innovator. Its Jeffersonian philosophy emphasized the desirability of decentralized decision-making and minimized the role of the professional administrators, including the manager.[26]

Further, one scholar who examined the politics of large council-manager cities argues that the demise of councilmanic participation in budget making is greatly exaggerated:

Nearly two-thirds of the managers reported that their councils gave detailed attention to three or more programs. In only three cities (7 percent) did the managers indicate that no program areas were subjected to detailed scrutiny. These results run counter to the pro forma or rubber stamp view of council budget consideration.[27]

Also, as one writer observes,[28] and the reader can no doubt substantiate in cities near him, individual councilmen may become leaders in specific areas of concern to them. Perhaps the most important factor relating to councilmanic involvement in policy development is the intensity of concern councilmen have for policy matters. Certainly, there are numerous examples of councils whose members are well paid and have substantial formal authority, but do not play an active role in policy development.

Even more so than is the case with most other actors examined in this book, there is little understanding of the variables that cause greater or lesser council participation in policy making. Few councils, however, play an important role in policy development.[29]

Policy Implementation

Here, as in the case of state legislators, city legislators appear to be at their nadir. For instance, Connecticut councilmen are very unlikely to be interested in administrative oversight, unless a question of patronage is involved.[30] Most councils lack the resources, as well as the will, necessary to oversee administration. In particular, there is the almost universal absence of professional staff, without whom it is impossible for urban legislators to learn much about the city bureaucracy.

There are variations, of course. While the manager form of government expressly prohibits council involvement in administrative matters, one study shows that this rule does not hold in a number of Florida communities where the council is concerned with the policy implementation process.[31] The Seattle city council is one example of a municipal legislature that plays an important role in policy implementation. Its members are well paid and are organized into standing committees, which exercise substantial control over the line departments. Committee chairmen maintain close liaison with department heads, who frequently consult with them on departmental matters.[32] Through the use of investigations and the auditing power, a council can have great impact on city administration.[33]

Conclusions more sophisticated than the above cannot be drawn because the requisite research does not exist. Hopefully, future research will provide a better idea of the conditions under which the council comes to play an active or a passive role in policy implementation.

Conclusion

Legislatures are much more handicapped in dealing with the bureaucracy than are chief executives, principally because they are not full-time institutions equipped with the resources to maintain continuing contact with administrative agencies. The example of a number of legislatures indicates that this situation is not inevitable, but rather the result of the way legislators define their role. If a large number of legislatures redefine their mission, the legislative branch can have substantial impact on the bureaucracy.

COURTS

Bureaucrats not only execute policy and "legislate" by making regulations, they also serve as judges. Any agency whose function is to regulate some aspect of behavior—and this includes most agencies—may become involved in administrative adjudication. A state public utilities commission, for example, may issue a new regulation concerning electricity rates that may then be challenged by either the power companies or a consumer group. At that point, the commission convenes as a court to hear the challenge. The plaintiff's lawyer argues the case and has the right to bring up and question witnesses. The commission's own legal staff presents its side, testimony is transcribed, and a decision is handed down. Hundreds of such proceedings occur every day, in which individuals argue before a draft board, welfare department, unemployment compensation board, tax department, zoning commission, and so on, that a ruling or regulation should be modified or reversed.

There are myriad variations in the structure of administrative courts. Many agencies have a built-in, standing court structure: zoning boards often have zoning boards of appeals, with a totally different membership; other agencies may simply designate their head or heads to act as judges; and in some cases a specially appointed examiner or administrative judge may hear the case and render a decision.   Only after the administrative agency has delivered its own verdict can either party bring the case to the judiciary, and only a small minority of such cases goes to the courts on appeal. The agencies themselves, acting as courts, settle most controversies concerning the agency.   Since most agency judicial decisions are never appealed to the judiciary, one must conclude that the weight of the agencies in adjudication rivals that of the judiciary. To be sure, the agencies are guided and constrained by pronouncements of the judiciary, but so are lower courts influenced by higher courts. And no authority on the judiciary would claim that lower courts lack substantial autonomy.[34]

It should be noted that this section is brief because there is almost no literature on the relation of the courts to executive branch policy making. Shapiro's work, which surveys the federal government alone, is virtually the only exception.[35]

Policy Development

While bureaucrats do most of their own adjudication, the courts play an important role in agency policy making. In this section and that on policy implementation, the impact of federal, state, and municipal courts on state and city agencies is examined.[36]

The impact of the judiciary on agency policy development can be enormous, as rulings on educational agencies demonstrate. Federal court decisions in the last twenty years have resulted in the integration of hundreds of formerly segregated schools and the banning of prayer in the public schools.[37] Repeated attempts to give financial aid to private religious schools have been struck down by federal courts. The California Supreme Court and other state courts have declared that the property tax is an unconstitutional means of public school support.

At the same time, the judiciary is constrained in several ways that do not apply to other political actors examined in this book. First, the courts are limited in that they are dependent upon other parties to initiate cases before they can render any kind of input into the decision-making process. Second, the power that the courts wield is almost entirely negative. They can overturn the acts of administrators and legislators, but they are rarely in a position to substitute their own ruling. Rather, they remand a matter to the original decision makers, with instructions to do it a different way.[38] Third, there are broad areas of activity in which courts are unlikely to intervene. They cannot accept cases asking review of agency behavior solely on the ground that it is inefficient or incompetent, for example, as can chief executives and legislatures. Their only concern must be whether the behavior in question is illegal or unconstitutional. Thus, broad areas of public policy are off limits. It is very difficult for the courts to review the behavior of planning, research, or overhead agencies, for example, since citizens are unlikely to be directly affected by the activities of these bureaus and are thus unable to bring suit against them.

It seems most likely that judicial power vis-à-vis bureaus is at its peak when the bureaus directly regulate some area of human behavior, whether it be land development, law enforcement, or receipt of welfare benefits. At this point, however, because research is lacking, it is possible only to pose questions about which types of agencies are most likely to be affected by which kinds of judicial action under which sorts of conditions.

Policy Implementation

Courts seem to be just as important in policy implementation as in policy development, as can be seen by a look at their caseloads. One study found that a very high proportion of urban trial court cases has to do with administrative agency decisions, such as zoning board actions on appeals for variances. Many of the cases dealt with appeals—suits or injunctions—by those who were adversely affected; the vast majority were initiated by individuals or businesses rather than interest groups or agencies.[39] In this manner the courts serve as an important check on the bureaucracy. In 1972 a federal court ordered Alabama state prison authorities to take immediate steps to provide adequate medical care for all inmates, noting that the administrators "have clearly abused their discretion."[40] Courts have temporarily taken over the operation of enterprises such as the bankrupt New Haven railroad.

Another look at educational agencies shows that courts have had considerable impact in recent years on public school disciplinary codes. In the past, students who disobeyed school regulations concerning dress, hair, and political activity were suspended, expelled, or otherwise punished. Today, students have appealed such disciplinary measures, and the courts have often sustained them, thus forcing changes in regulations.

A fundamental limitation on judicial influence in policy implementation is the courts' dependence on bureaucrats to carry out decisions. The letter or spirit of the law is often evaded by bureaucrats confronted by court orders. One Southern school district that was told to desegregate its schools separated black and white children in its buses and justified this action as a safeguard against disorder. A series of court decisions has mandated an end to physical coercion or "third-degree" tactics in the interrogation of suspects and requires that suspects be informed of their constitutional rights to legal counsel, to refuse to answer questions, and so on. In many cases the directives have been ignored by police, who have continued to operate as they did before. The principal remedy an individual has against this kind of bureaucratic behavior is to go to court; bureaucrats can be brought to trial, and agencies can have injunctions issued against them. Although such cases undoubtedly involve only a tiny fraction of bureaucratic offenses, the prospect may serve to indirectly restrain some bureaucrats. However, the process is costly and time consuming, so most persons do not use it.

As is the case in judicial policy development, the question of which types of bureaus are most likely to be influenced by the courts in policy implementation, or under which kinds of conditions, remains unanswered. Great variations presumably exist, but students of the courts have for the most part ignored the bureaucracy, and students of the bureaucracy have ignored the courts.

Conclusion

While courts are definitely important in both policy development and implementation, they are constrained by factors which do not restrict other types of actors. Our present knowledge of the nature of court-bureau influence relationships is minimal.

CHAPTER FOUR

Political Parties

We must define our terms before we discuss the relationship between political parties and policy making, because although the primary goal of parties is to win control of the government, there are different concepts of the word "party."

Party in the electorate. This concept refers to those who are registered members of a party, or those who vote for candidates of a party in an election.

Party in the government. Most officeholders at all levels of government are members of either the Republican or the Democratic party. The term "party in the government" refers to these officeholders.

Party organization. This term includes all those who work within the party organization itself, as it manifests itself in town, city, county, and state committees.

While one person can simultaneously play more than one party role, discussion in this chapter is concerned with the party organization and its leaders and the variables that affect their policy-making power.

POLICY DEVELOPMENT

State Government

The primary goal of party organization leaders is victory in the next election. Depending upon the political environment in which they find themselves, party leaders take different stances when considering whether to urge their nominees to stress certain kinds of issues during and after the campaign.

One issue of great concern to all party leaders is proposed changes in election laws, for the formal structure of representation is never a neutral issue. Different parties and party leaders will have varying chances to win under alternative structures. A change in state legislative district boundaries, for example, if accomplished adroitly enough, can cause the majority party to switch places with the minority, even if its proportion of the total vote remains the same. The qualifications set for entrants in primary elections (the number of signatures on a petition, whether a certain percentage of delegate votes at the party convention is needed, and so on) can determine if the choice of organization leaders will be challenged. Since these matters are fundamental to the good health of the party organization, it is no surprise that they are paramount concerns of party leaders.

In much of the country, party leaders seem interested in only one type of issue besides those relating to electoral structure: that which seems very likely to affect the outcome of an election. For example, George McGovern found himself pressed by state and city party leaders to change his position on welfare, defense, and amnesty during his 1972 presidential campaign. They felt that his views were so unpopular that he would not only lose the election but also drag down with himself a host of candidates for state and city offices. Former Democratic National Chairman John M. Bailey, also Connecticut state chairman, once appeared on television with his Republican counterpart, Congressman William Miller. Their debate revealed that Bailey did not know very much about current leading issues, and when the show ended, Bailey complained that his opponent had taken an unfair tack in stressing issues. Bailey freely admitted that he was not issue-oriented but, rather, concerned with winning votes. This writer has listened to a number of Northeastern party leaders explain their belief that the public has little interest in most issues and that they must therefore enhance a candidate's image, coach him on television style, and assemble an efficient organization.

Americans like to use the terms "conservative" and "liberal" when talking politics, but often these terms descriptive of ideological stances simply have no relevance in distinguishing the two parties at the city and state level. Political attacks on each other by Republicans and Democrats are usually couched in personal phraseology—wisdom, moral probity, and ties to selfish interests—rather than based on any substantive policy orientation.

In some areas of the country, party leaders seem much more attentive to substantive issues, supporting candidates who think as they do rather than necessarily supporting those who they feel have the best chance to win. In states where the reform movement has been historically strong, such as California, Wisconsin, and Minnesota, party leaders are more likely to be issue-oriented. In these states, not as much patronage exists as in some other states, so party leaders may have to stress issues to get campaign workers, since they cannot offer much material incentive. However, the patronage-reform dichotomy does not explain all or perhaps even most of the variation in issue orientation among party leaders. That is, some party leaders who can offer patronage incentives may still stress substantive issues, while leaders who have little patronage to offer may shy away from issues. Because very little information is available on overall patterns, the question of which variables are the key ones must remain moot.

City Government

The electoral system at the local level is often unlike that at the state level, since many cities and towns do not have partisan elections. In a non-partisan election there are no party labels—no Democrats, no Republicans, no assorted third parties—on the ballot. Candidates run as individuals, although they may be endorsed by various civic groups. Nonpartisan elections do not obtain at the national level, or at the state level, with the exception of those for the Minnesota and Nebraska legislatures. Thus, they are for all practical purposes a unique attribute of American city government.

Nonpartisan elections are an integral plank in the platform of the municipal reform movement and were designed to separate local politics from the influence of party organizations. The reformers were motivated by a basic conviction that political parties (or "machines") and party leaders (or "bosses") were a baneful presence in government and society. The remedy was to take partisan politics out of government; then government could be run by upright middle-class citizens and competent professionals who would produce policy in the public interest. Although all the reformers' hopes and predictions of more honest and efficient government have not been realized,[1] they have won their campaign to institutionalize nonpartisan electoral systems; today two-thirds of American cities over five thousand population have such systems.[2]

The existence of a nonpartisan electoral system does not mean that party leaders are unimportant political figures. Certainly this is *not* the case in cities like Boston and Chicago, which have nonpartisan electoral systems,[3] but in many of the newer cities of the Southwest and far West, there really is no one like the professional party politician in the older, more settled areas. In many California cities, for example, politics is nonpartisan in fact as well as name.[4] While politics exists, the local Democratic and Republican organizations are not important actors in local elections. In their place are good government groups of the type that back the reform movement, ad hoc coalitions of community groups, and, sometimes, simply electoral chaos in which every candidate runs independently and there is no continuity from one election to the next. Thus, in a sizeable minority of American cities, party leaders are not a force in local politics.

City party leaders display the same kind of variations in orientation toward policy as their state counterparts. There are noticeable differences in stress on substantive issues between issue-oriented reformers, whether in New York, Los Angeles, or Chicago, and patronage-oriented party leaders. Because of the greater popularity of reform institutions at the local level, there may be more reform party leaders there than at the state level, though no exact count has been made.

Both reform and patronage-oriented city politicians share the concern of state party chiefs about election laws and issues that may determine the outcome of elections. In 1955, for example, a New York City Republican leader criticized his party's state legislators, who wanted to relax rent control regulations. He warned that if the proposal were to become law, the Republican city vote would be affected "tremendously."[5] Party leaders often oppose plans for highways or urban renewal that would raze entire neighborhoods, for there are many votes in those neighborhoods.

What relationship exists between state and city party leaders and bureaucrats in the policy development process? This depends on the issue orientation of the party leader. If he is highly issue-oriented, he will need information from bureaucrats, or from other actors such as legislators who obtain it from bureaucrats. On matters of great popular concern, party leaders are not so likely to need this kind of information. Rather, they are interested principally in taking a public stand. In many instances, indeed, they need no help from bureaucrats, whether the subject is abortion-law change, greater penalties for drug pushers, or the path a highway should take. The party leader usually leaves finding the exact policy remedies to other actors, to the legislators and chief executives. He is content to raise and discuss a problem, and demand, in general terms, that something be done. Party leaders do not generally need bureaucratic advice on election-law issues, because this is a policy area with which they are familiar. Given the relatively narrow focus of their policy development interest, then, most party leaders are probably not dependent upon bureaucrats. However, the minority of party leaders who are oriented toward substantive issues are much more in need of informational aid from bureaucrats than are the majority of party leaders.

POLICY IMPLEMENTATION

State Government

When a party wins an election, party leaders need to reward campaign workers. To do so, they must have control over or influence with executive branch agencies,[6] and the chances are that the executive branch will be responsive to their demands. What they desire most often makes their relationship with the agencies uneasy and awkward: concessions or exceptions for their supporters, something that is bound to add to the difficulties in the day-to-day job of the career administrator. For example, one category of favors is government jobs. A party worker may want such a job whether or not he has the requisite skills. If he is incompetent, career bureaucrats will be unhappy to accept him as a new employee of the agency. A second category of favors is government contracts. Enormous sums of money are involved in contracts awarded by urban and state governments, and party leaders want to be sure of a share for the party faithful, regardless of how agency heads may feel. Finally, but quite important to the party leaders, is exceptions for constituents: fixing a traffic ticket, procuring welfare for an applicant who might be technically ineligible but nonetheless in need, and obtaining a scholarship for a college student. Party leaders are especially desirous of all these favors to cement the relationship between them and their followers. Career bureaucrats, on the other hand, resist infringements of the rules under which they function.

In 1968, some 58 percent of state government employees were under merit systems.[7]   The true extent of coverage is no doubt significantly smaller, because there are ways of evading merit requirements. For example, since the chief executive usually appoints the members of the commission overseeing the merit system, he may be able to pack the body with persons of minimal commitment to the principles at stake. Second, under most merit systems, the "rule of three" prevails; that is, for any given position, one need not select the highest-scoring individual, but one among the top three. This feature is designed to promote flexibility, but it can also be used to promote those who have served the party. Third, many state governments have a large number of employees who enter on a "temporary" basis, thus avoiding an examination, but who somehow come to spend a long time in state service.[8]

How does one go about applying for a job in state agencies not under the merit system? A recent article dealing with patronage in Indiana serves as an illustration. A twenty-five-year-old Vietnam veteran wanted to work for the state highway department and was told that the only qualification, which he met, was Republican registration. In addition to the usual questions, the application asked, "How long have you been a member of the Republican party?" and "Would you be willing to contribute regularly to the Indiana Republican State Central Committee?" The completed form, along with endorsement from party organization leaders in his area, was forwarded to Republican state headquarters for further processing. The "voluntary" party contribution expected of a patronage employee is 2 percent of his salary, and retaining his job is contingent upon donation.[9] The Indiana arrangement is unique only in the candor with which it is acknowledged; kickback schemes are common. In Illinois and Ohio, for example, they are termed "flower funds," a name derived from the politicians' custom of sending flowers to funerals and wakes. Patronage employees can also expect to participate in such fund-raising devices as testimonial dinners.[10]

Even in a state like New York, which has a merit system, there are many patronage posts in the executive branch. In 1968 there were 1,050 exempt from merit coverage; 24,600 noncompetitive; and 14,000 provisional. The exempt jobs are so-called "political" or policy-making appointments, such as commissioners and their aides; the noncompetitive positions include, among others, inspectors and examiners, which are considered difficult to test; provisional posts are "temporary" slots in agencies like the antipoverty program.[11]

New York is not alone. Georgia Highway Commissioner Jim Gillis is responsible for deciding which banks receive millions of dollars in state highway fund deposits. It is no surprise to find that those banks which have helped the commissioner and his political allies are awarded accounts.[12]

Under Governor George Wallace, the Alabama highway department built roads where his supporters wanted them. The governor made sure that his friends were materially remembered and that others were ignored. As state highway director E. N. Rogers wrote to an engineering firm, explaining why it could not secure state business, "Frankly, on what interstate work we are contracting, I have a list from the governor's office from which I am supposed to make my selections." Wallace's brother Gerald has prospered through state contracts.[13]

City Government

Generally speaking, civil service coverage is a function of size: all cities over one million population in 1966 had a civil service commission of some kind, while only 84 percent of cities between one hundred thousand and one million had such a commission.[14] Certain jobs are much more likely than others to be outside civil service coverage; a 1962 survey showed these amounted to almost 46 percent of full-time municipal employment and usually included most employees working in the areas of highways, health, hospitals, sewage, sanitation, and parks and recreation.[15]

Although most political scientists agree that the number of patronage positions in urban government has declined greatly in the twentieth century, there is evidence that with the proliferation of new government programs since 1964 there has been an increase in such positions in certain policy areas. A 1968 report states that New York's Mayor Robert Wagner had at his disposal from 1953 to 1965 $10 million in jobs exempt from civil service. In 1968, his successor, Mayor John Lindsay, had $33 million in exempt jobs in poverty agencies alone, while the city's provisional employees had increased from 1,500 to 12,800. Lindsay, widely known as a reform mayor, gave top-ranking positions in his administration to fifteen of the sixteen borough coordinators of his election campaign. Such behavior is recognition of the functional necessity of rewarding those who help an official to be elected. Mayor Erastus Corning of Albany, New York, is president of a firm that receives $100,000 annually in premiums for insuring the property of Albany County. The matter was concluded without bids, because by law rates are fixed by the state insurance department, and no insurance company may compete with another in pricing.[16]

Wolfinger's study of New Haven politics indicates the nature and extent of patronage politics in a medium-sized northeastern city (150,000) with a civil service system. Wolfinger counted 75 political or policy-making appointments, 300 lower-level patronage jobs, and about 300 appointments to various citizen boards and commissions. In addition, each year the city hires 100-150 young men for temporary unskilled jobs, mainly with the parks, public works, and parking departments. A number of positions are to be found in the county sheriff's office, the field offices of state government, the city court, and New Haven probate court. In addition, Wolfinger notes the importance of private patronage, that is, the hiring by business-men closely related to the party in power of a person recommended by the politicians. New Haven, then, like the governments discussed above, is able to remember materially the party faithful. In return, patronage appointees are assessed a percentage of their salary. Besides receiving contributions from companies who are awarded government contracts, the party organization can often procure substantial sums from activities stringently regulated by the city. As Wolfinger asserts, the construction business, for example, is a political business, because there is much public building and because the city regulates it in so many ways. He notes that the larger contractors, while associated with one party, usually give heavily to both.[17]

Not all city governments have this kind of patronage politics. In contrast with patronage-oriented systems are those reform governments in some areas of the western United States that have neither much patronage nor strong party organization leaders. No doubt, favors and exceptions are made in these political systems, but they are not made at the behest of party leaders who are not very important figures in local politics.

Some analysts believe that machine patronage-oriented politics serves to coordinate fragmented urban government:

> The key structural function of the Boss is to organize, centralize and maintain in good working condition the "scattered fragments of power" which are at present dispersed through our political organization, the municipal government. By the centralized organization of political power, the Boss and his apparatus can satisfy the needs of diverse sub-groups in a larger community which are not politically satisfied by legally devised and culturally approved social structures.[18]

In other words, control of the party machinery may enable politicians to coordinate the multitude of agencies legally independent from the chief executive. As noted in Chapter 2, Mayor Lee of New Haven was able to exert a great deal of influence over the boards of aldermen, zoning appeals, and finance, in large part because he was a strong enough party leader to deny renomination to dissidents.

Wolfinger disputes the contention that the machine brings about policy coordination, arguing that there is no necessary relationship between strong party organizations based on patronage and centralization of political power. As noted in Chapter 2, he says that the decision-making role of "Boss" Richard Daley consists more of mediating conflict than of espousing a policy viewpoint, and that this should be no surprise, since Daley's main interest as party leader is to win elections—local, state, or national—rather than to coordinate policy. If anything, a concern with policy coordination is likely to hurt the party organization for two reasons: first, the party will no longer be able to remain neutral on policy issues; second, its need for favors and exceptions will inevitably interfere with any attempt to bring about centralized administration.[19]   Coordination in policy implementation must come from a source other than the party organization.

Conclusion

Although there are variations in the behavior and power of party leaders at the various levels of government, some generalizations can be made about their behavior. These hypotheses certainly do not cover all party leaders, yet they seem to hold true for most. In any case, more research is needed before these generalizations can be definitively accepted or rejected.

Party leaders are influential actors in the policy implementation process. They are often able to receive the different kinds of favors and exceptions that they want from administrators. They are usually not so important in the policy development process, however, except in the area of election law. When it comes to other types of policy development decisions, they are often apathetic. Thus, party leaders have an uneven impact on policy making: they are more active in policy implementation than in policy development.

Further, the nature of party leaders' demands places fundamental restrictions on the scope of their involvement in policy implementation. Their focus is quite narrow: favors and exceptions from the bureaucracy, rather than substantive policy preferences. As a result, party leaders are unlikely to have the same impact on policy making as chief executives, career bureaucrats, the legislature, and interest groups, even when all their demands are satisfied, which rarely happens. This situation is due to the very nature of the needs of the organizations party leaders run. Thus, although they are political actors whose power is not to be discounted, their activity, both actual and potential, is more limited than that of most other actors examined in this book.

CHAPTER FIVE

Interest Groups and Employee Unions

INTEREST GROUPS AND BUREAUS

Any kind of nongovernmental association of a voluntary nature can be considered an interest group if and when it becomes politically active. Thus, the National Rifle Association, the Grange, the Teamsters Union, the Chamber of Commerce, the American Association of University Professors, and the Roman Catholic Church are all interest groups when they become involved in attempts to influence the policy-making process in areas of concern to them.

The range of possible relationships between executive branch bureaus and interest groups is wide and can be illustrated by two typologies developed by Wallace Sayre.[1] Both typologies picture interest groups who are vitally concerned with the politics of a particular agency as the clientele or the constituency of the agency. That is, farm groups are the clientele of a department of agriculture; patients and their families, the clientele of a department of mental health; and the electrical and telephone industries, the clientele of a public utilities commission. Staff and overhead agencies have a clientele composed of line agencies. The focus in this discussion is on line agencies and their interest group clientele.

The clientele of a bureau comprises those who are most directly affected by the bureau, who perceive this, and who organize to exert influence over the bureau. For example, the clientele of a health department bureau that inspects public places for conformity with health and sanitation codes are the public places themselves. They are most directly affected by the bureau's activities, because they can be penalized if they are in violation of the codes. While one could argue that their patrons are just as directly affected, the patrons' perception of the situation differs from that of the proprietors. Most patrons do not feel strongly enough about code violations—if, indeed, they are aware of many of them—to organize groups to pressure the bureau. The clientele of a bureau does not consist of all groups affected by the bureau's work, but those who are so affected and organize to influence the bureau. Groups affected by the bureau's work but who do not organize to influence the bureau, such as restaurant and hotel guests, can be referred to as potential clientele. At some time in the future, they may organize to influence the bureau, but at the present time they are politically quiescent.

Bureaus and their interest group constituency form an interdependent partnership. The bureau would not exist if it had no clientele to serve, and the bureau's clientele are significantly affected by the activities of the bureau. Without people on welfare, welfare bureaucrats would be out of work. Without a welfare department, poor people might starve.

The first typology developed by Sayre focuses on the interest group clientele of an agency. Making an analogy with state party electoral systems, he distinguishes among one-party, two-party, modified one-party, and multiparty interest group systems relative to an administrative agency.

The one-party system in state politics refers to a situation where one party enjoys a virtual monopoly in electoral victories. Likewise, there are many administrative agencies that can be said to have a one-party clientele. This does not necessarily mean that there is only one interest group attentive to the activities of the agency, but rather one type of group. To illustrate, the clientele of the Florida Department of Veterans' Affairs is exclusively composed of veterans' associations, such as the American Legion and Veterans of Foreign Wars, which share the same outlook on almost all agency policies.

A two-party system relative to an administrative agency is a competitive one, where two interest groups of roughly equal strength vie for influence over agency decisions. An example is the Vermont State Board of Health, which, on the one hand, confronts the Southern Vermont Environmental Council and associated conservationists favoring strict controls on land development and, on the other hand, the Common Sense Associates, a group of businessmen-developers who have urged a loosening of the board's strict land development regulations and have opposed strict enforcement.[2]

A modified one-party system exists where there are two types of interest groups actively concerned with an administrative agency's policies, and there is a noticeable disparity in their influence. Typically, one of the two prevails, but the second group may sometimes win, so that a pure one-party situation does not exist. The usual big-city police department is a good example of a contemporary modified one-party system. At this point in history, it is likely to be confronted by minority group critics who may be allied with liberal reformist groups. Alternatively, there are strong supporters of the police, perhaps including members of veterans' organizations, hard-hat labor union men, and staunch middle-class citizens. The second group is likely to be more influential but may not prevail all the time. The police may decide to establish informal review boards or consult subcommunity leaders on policy. If so, a modified one-party system exists.

Finally, some agencies have a multiparty constituency, where more than two parties are effective actors vis-à-vis the agency. Sayre and Kaufman describe the New York City school system as an agency with a multiparty constituency that includes religious groups, the Public Education Association, the Citizens Committee for Children, black groups, and local boards.[3]

Another way advanced by Sayre of conceptualizing the relationships between interest groups and administrative agencies is to look at the political strength that the agencies may derive from alliance with interest groups, that is, the nature of the potential support that the interest groups can give to the agency. The first category in this typology is the *underprivileged* agency, which cannot count on much support from its clientele. The New York City Fire Department falls in this category. Businesses subject to inspection and licensing do not like its activities; economy groups are cautious lest its budget be expanded too much; and the National Board of Fire Underwriters has endorsed recommendations for a reduction in the force.[4] Other examples in this category include welfare and correction agencies; neither people on welfare nor prisoners have much political influence.

A second type of relationship is one in which the agency is held *captive* by its interest group clientele. Such seems to be a frequent occurrence for state public utilities commissions, which are charged with regulating telephone and power companies. Most have never been known to show any crusading zeal on behalf of the consumer; rather, they tend to approve requests of the industries, whether in matters of rates or facilities.[5]

A third type of relationship—difficult to differentiate from the captive kind—is one in which the bureau is a *partner* of its interest group constituency, that is, a situation where both seem to enjoy roughly equal power and ties are extremely close. This often seems to be the case in state departments of education, where the state education association, which represents teachers in the public primary and secondary schools, has very close links with the agency itself. Often, there is a great deal of interchange between the staffs of the state association and the state agency dealing with primary and secondary education.

A large number of agencies whose employees are highly professionalized appear to be characterized by partner relationships. Professions are characterized by their own institutions of education, membership associations, and self-regulation. It is the medical, legal, educational, and social work professions themselves, for example, not government agencies, who determine standards of conduct and evaluation. In short, the professions are largely autonomous occupational groupings. They are relevant to this discussion in that they are often the dominant clientele of an agency—a profession may staff an agency and provide it with norms.

Such is almost always the case for health, education, and welfare, which constitute the bulk of subnational government activity, as measured in both employees and dollars. Harold Seidman calls these professional associations "self-governing guilds" that control agencies, and one must agree with him, because the interest group and the agency have become indistinguishable.[6] Social workers, for example, have determined the norms of welfare agencies for years, even under increasing criticism from welfare recipients.[7]   Recently, Connecticut's welfare workers publicly censured the new Commissioner of Welfare for the first time. They did so not because he had worked steadily to reduce welfare benefits, but because he had the temerity to suggest that neighborhood welfare recipients might be as effective social workers as the professionally trained person.[8] The guilds are key interest groups for many agencies and play a very important role in the federal system.

Finally, some agencies are in the position of *leader* vis-à-vis their clientele. It is the agency itself that initiates most policy changes and is able to win the support of its clientele for them. Such a condition may characterize some state police department–local police department relations.

Thus, the possible range of relationships of interest groups and administrative agencies is very broad, and it is difficult to generalize about the subject. The same is true of the relationships between the two typologies. One might think that all one-party systems relate to captive agencies, but they may equally well characterize partner or leader relationships. A multiparty constituency could characterize both an underprivileged and a leader relationship. The only way to determine the relationship is to investigate a specific agency, and even then it may be exceedingly difficult to distinguish among captive, partner, or leader relationships on anything other than an intuitive basis. These rubrics have analytical utility, however, in the absence of better typologies and data. Very little research on city and state bureau-clientele relationships exists, and more information is necessary for an understanding of the behavioral patterns in this interaction.

Policy Development

Since there are thousands of interest groups at the city and state levels, it is especially hazardous to generalize about their behavior. There are several variables that seem to relate to interest group success, including organization, money, access to governmental decision makers, the ability to articulate and defend a position, and political skill. If an interest group has all of these resources, it will be an unusually effective actor; if it has none, it will be impotent.

A well-organized group can mobilize its members to confront not only bureau officials but other political actors who can influence the bureau. If it has money, it can finance a variety of campaigns to bring attention to itself and its goals. If it has access to government officials because of past or present interaction with them, it has an advantage over groups who are strangers to the officials. If it can expound its arguments logically and forcefully, it is in a better position than groups who protest but fail to give clear expositions of their grievances. Finally, if it is politically skillful, the group knows whom to see, how to conduct itself in bargaining, and which tactics maximize its goals.

If an interest group exploits these assets, it is likely to enjoy a close relationship to bureau officials. This relationship will manifest itself in frequent consultation about policy, collaboration in drafting policy development proposals, and joint action to attempt to bring about alliances with other political actors. This kind of cooperation characterizes bureaus that are the captive, partner, or leader of their clientele, as well as bureaus with a one-party or modified one-party interest group constituency. These close relationships are a function of the strength or cumulative resources of the interest group, or, in the case of a leader bureau, the strength of the bureau.

When an interest group lacks some of these five resources, it is likely to find itself the clientele of an underprivileged bureau, in a multiparty bureau constituency, or the lesser party in a modified one-party system. In such positions it probably will not work closely with the bureau in policy development. As a result, it may try to gain a voice in policy by attempting to influence other actors; it may present proposals directly to the legislature, or try to lobby chief executives. Catholic groups, for example, unable to win the support of state departments of education for subsidies to parochial schools, have frequently persuaded legislatures to adopt these proposals. In this fashion, a group lacking only bureau access may compensate with access to another actor.

Two-party bureau constituencies may be made up of groups with all five resources or of groups lacking some or all of them. The existence of a two-party system indicates that the bureau clientele are evenly matched. In this case, once again, a key determinant in the success of each interest group "party" may be the access it has to other actors.

Policy Implementation

The interest group clientele of a bureau is concerned as much with policy implementation as with policy development, and the resources discussed above have just as much impact in determining influence in policy implementation as in policy development. In this section, the emphasis is on the strategies interest groups follow to maximize their influence in policy implementation.[9]

A bureau's clientele seeks the organizational location most favorable to both bureau and clientele. Most bureaus could be located in several places; for example, a mental retardation treatment center might be placed in a department of health, department of mental health, or department of hospitals. The interest group wants to make sure that the bureau is located in the department likely to be most sympathetic to its programs and budget requests. Further, the interest group that develops a close relationship to the agency may try to assure it of as much legal autonomy as possible by having it removed from the chief executive's chain of command.

An interest group prefers that the bureau have a one-party constituency so it will not have to contend with other interest groups for bureau influence. The goal of this strategy is to attain a virtual monopoly over access to the agency. The interest group moves to attain this goal by having assigned to an agency only those functions of concern to it. Other functions are removed so there is no competition with other interest groups for the agency's budget and programs. That many interest groups have been successful in this kind of strategy is shown by the proliferation of city and state agencies, many of which are integrally related but administratively separate. This interest group goal explains why chief executives are usually opposed by bureau clientele in their efforts to reorganize and combine agencies and thereby to create agencies with two-party or multiparty constituencies. An attempt to include the structurally autonomous state Fisheries and Game Board under the Massachusetts Department of Conservation, for example, was opposed by sportsmen's groups.[10] An exception to this pattern may occur when a bureau and its clientele are so weak that they feel they have everything to gain and nothing to lose by a consolidating reorganization, which might possibly result in their enlistment of the new departmental commissioner as an ally.

Bureau clientele groups work toward the creation of bureau advisory units and "pack" them with their own representatives. All but the smallest bureaus in state governments and larger cities are likely to have at least one advisory body attached to them. A department of environmental protection, for example, may have advisory groups dealing with air pollution, water pollution, soil conservation, and the like. The "advisory" group often has more than advisory power. It may have a statutory basis for existence, as well as its own professional staff. Sometimes the agency must have the approval of the advisory group before it can make decisions in certain policy areas or install a new chief. By creating and peopling an advisory unit, then, bureau clientele can become a part of the bureau itself.

Another way for the clientele to fuse itself organizationally with the bureau is to gain a voice in the staffing of the agency. Interest groups may attempt to affect the staffing of an agency not only by advancing their own candidates for agency head but also by recommending graduates of favored schools or transferring their own employees to the rolls of the agency. If interest groups are notably successful in this effort, the bureau is sure to be either a captive or partner of its clientele. Indeed, it will be difficult to tell the bureau and its clientele apart—they may be a functional unity.

Conclusion

Interest groups are not the alpha and omega of politics. One survey of small-town city managers found that one-fourth of them were never even approached by community interest groups.[11] It is impossible to understand the politics of administrative agencies, however, without an understanding of the nature of their clientele groups. The organization, resources, and political skill of clientele determine, to a great extent, the power that a bureau has.

EMPLOYEE UNIONS

As the author of one study of federal bureaucratic politics has noted, the two groups most concerned with bureau policies are clientele groups and the agency's own employees.[12] Although bureaucrats have already been discussed at length, it is appropriate to elaborate here on one of the most striking recent developments in city and state government: the growth of employee unions.

The president of the American Federation of State, County, and Municipal Employees, AFL-CIO (AFSCME) has referred to the growth of government unionism as a "revolution." Certainly, the rate of expansion of government unions has been meteoric: the AFSCME doubled in size between 1965 and 1970, growing to 600,000 members.[13] One-quarter of all state and local government employees now belong to a union or employee association. Half of all state and local bureaucrats work in states that give them collective bargaining rights, or the right to sit down with government to negotiate the terms of their contracts. Strikes have become commonplace: in 1958, only 7,510 man-days of work were lost as a result of bureaucratic strikes, while the number rose to over 2.5 million by 1968.[14]

Unions command impressive resources to wield in decisions affecting them. First, in many cities, their members have enough votes to swing a close election. In cities like New York, their influence is maximized because of this resource. Mayor John Lindsay fought the union leaders during the initial part of his first term, but as the date for reelection drew near, he became close friends with them. During that election year there were no major strikes, and the unions received handsome contracts for their members.[15]

Second, unions can paralyze a city if they go on strike. Without garbage pickups, bus or subway service, or schools, a city is at a serious disadvantage. Labor solidarity is a related resource, since private sector unions may honor picket lines around city jails or schools.[16] Unions, then, are a force to be reckoned with. How does their influence manifest itself in the different states of the policy-making process?

Policy Development

Government unions, like their private sector counterparts, are interested primarily in bread-and-butter issues and the nature of their working environment. They are more concerned with pay, fringe benefits, working conditions, and grievances of individual members than with broad questions of policy. There are unions that have demanded a voice in the making of key decisions, however, and even those unions that do not make such demands have great impact on the nature and scope of governmental decision making because of the effect of their other demands.

In New York City, which is in the vanguard of new developments in almost all aspects of American society, welfare workers struck in 1965, demanding that their clients be given twice-yearly clothing grants, telephone allowances, and a 25 percent budget increase. While the welfare workers did not win these demands, the New York City teachers' union was able to stop school decentralization through a 1967 strike and subsequent lobbying with the state legislature.

Although there has so far been little demand by unions for a voice in policy development, no doubt the demand will increase in the future. There are limits to union influence in this area, though, because public unions recognize government officials as management, just as private sector unions recognize business as management. Both types of unions acknowledge that policy development is the sphere of management, not labor, although labor will immediately object to management actions affecting employee work conditions.[17] But unions do not want the responsibility of running a community, according to David Stanley, a leading authority on the subject. Stanley argues that they need an adversary, someone to be management to their labor. This factor is the most important check on union influence in policy making.[18]

The indirect effects of union agreements have profound implications for policy development. Each time a union achieves a settlement guaranteeing more money for less work, the government has less resources to devote to programs of all kinds. A former budget director of New York City argues that unions have made the job of the budget director "almost impossible,"[19] since financial planning for government programs cannot be carried out when the results of labor negotiations cannot be anticipated, and the result of these negotiations may force a shift in funds from one program to another.

While there are basic constraints on union power in policy development, no one should underestimate this power. Further, this power is certain to increase in the future as unions recruit more members and grow in political experience.

Policy Implementation

The impact of unions in policy implementation is profound, and far more important than in policy development. Concern with the working conditions of members causes the union to become interested in all areas of work.

Unions demand a voice in determining case workloads, how many employees are assigned to each job, which shifts workers are assigned to, which workers get overtime, what kind of work an employee must do, work locations, and safety conditions. One study of municipal unions in nineteen communities found that unions are chiefly interested in these kinds of concerns, plus pay and grievances, while they are less interested in hiring, promotion, training, and classification.

The cumulative impact of union pressures in these areas limits the managerial discretion of political executives. They no longer have the authority to specify exactly how an order is carried out in many areas. For example, a fireman may refuse to do repair work because it is not part of his job classification. Today, department heads must devote much more time to negotiating, allocating equipment, determining assignments, and adjusting grievances than they did before the advent of unions.[20]

In addition, legislatures and chief executives have become preoccupied with union matters. If a strike is on or imminent, these officials will be primarily concerned with it, to the exclusion of other matters. Even if collective bargaining results in an agreement that averts a strike, the settlement may precipitate a crisis in finance or public relations if it is an economically costly one.

As Stanley points out, even if a strike does not threaten, officials must devote a substantial amount of resources to personnel problems. Union delegations visit legislators and the chief executive, who must spend more time on labor relations problems with the personnel office and department heads. When dozens of different unions are active, as is the case in larger cities, the problem is multiplied.[21]

In short, where unions exist, political executives must share control over policy implementation with them, as well as the other actors discussed in this book.

Conclusion

Government unions are here to stay and will wield increasing power in future policy making. At present, their influence in policy implementation overshadows their influence in policy development, but union power in both areas will continue to grow.

CHAPTER SIX

Communications Media and Advisory Groups

COMMUNICATIONS MEDIA

Any treatment of the communications media must distinguish among types. The focus here is primarily on mass media, which reach very large numbers of people, rather than on elite media, which appeal to much smaller numbers of people in leadership groups. The mass media can be divided into two broad categories: printed (newspapers and magazines) and electronic (television and radio). This discussion deals primarily with the press, because there has been very little substantive research done on the political behavior of television and radio reporters, and there is no reason to believe that their behavior is very different from that of press reporters. In addition, the electronic media seem unlikely to play as great a part in the politics of many cities and states as do newspapers. Smaller cities, in particular, are much less likely to have television stations than they are to have newspapers, and radio stations spend very little time on local news.[1]

Media and Executive Branch

The newspaper press is the only actor in city and state politics, other than the chief executive, to take a comprehensive view. Reporters are likely to be interested in any part of the government, which is not true of most other actors, who are usually concerned with just a few agencies. Reporters pursue a story only if it conforms to their definition of news. Several studies have found that they believe readers like certain kinds of stories more than others, which is why they concentrate on material dealing with conflict, change, the unique, and names. Reporters pay attention to all kinds of controversy, violent or not, and it is inconceivable that the media would regularly play up harmony on college campuses or in city halls and state capitols when such is the case. Any kind of obvious change or departure, such as a new drug rehabilitation program, is reported. Unique events of human interest, such as a bureau head's volunteering to spend time in jail to better appreciate what prisoners experience, are given prominence. Names are news because reporters believe readers respond to a "star system," as do fans of rock or opera. For example, one study (see footnote 2) quotes a reporter as saying that he "would never snub the governor, regardless of how important events occurring elsewhere were," when the chief executive called a press conference or asked to see newsmen.

These focuses have profound implications for the way in which news is covered. Rarely is there consideration of the background to a story, or an attempt to probe deeply into its meaning. As likely as not, the reporter will be writing on another subject the next day, so that his approach is descriptive rather than analytical. In addition, he is under pressure to meet deadlines and lacks time to reflect and write in depth, which results in superficiality, uniformity, and discontinuity of coverage.[2] These statements do not imply in any way that reporters are inferior or shallow persons; they simply point out the constraints placed on reporters by the nature of their work. Reporters often write very differently when they are not writing for newspapers, as Rowland Evans and Robert Novak's books on Lyndon Johnson and Richard Nixon demonstrate.

Superficiality, uniformity, and discontinuity characterize media reporting of any level of government, but they are especially notable on the city and state levels. The state level of government seems to be an indeterminate one of which people are not very conscious; they relate much more readily to either the local or the national government.[3] Wisconsin statehouse reporters feel that readers are both ignorant of and uninterested in state government: "You try to think of the questions [readers] could or would raise—sometimes these are dumb questions—you write as though they know very little."[4] Newspapers usually pay less attention to local than to national developments, and where they give each equal billing, in cities like Cleveland, Detroit, and St. Louis, papers are economically well-off. One study concludes that, "in the few cities where newspapers are really competitive, the coverage of local government is conspicuously thin. Crime and sensation, human interest, and circulation-building contests tend to take the place of serious coverage of local news in these cities."[5]

Reporter and Government Official

Representatives of the news media may often enter into conflict with government officials, who are greatly concerned with media coverage and who attempt to have themselves pictured in the best possible light. Today government agencies of any size have public relations offices that, whatever their designation, crank out reams of releases and information for the media. In some cases, imaginative use of public relations techniques can result in great dividends for the agency. A study of the New Haven antipoverty program describes such efforts, which made the program the "showcase" of national antipoverty programs.[6]

In spite of even the most brilliant public relations, the relationship between government officials and reporters is often antagonistic, because the goals of each group differ when it comes to the dissemination of information. Reporters want to know as much as possible about government and want to emphasize conflict. The more stories they produce that highlight controversy, the more likely they are to be featured on the front page, become widely known, and be promoted. Government officials, on the other hand, want to keep private as many matters within their purview as possible to enhance their ability to influence the decision-making process. If a policy development proposal under consideration becomes public knowledge, it will maximize the opportunity for potential opponents of the project to mobilize. In addition, officials may often be trying to cover up practices, legal or illegal, that may prove embarrassing to them. Thus, they try to hide many potential news items, while reporters tend to exaggerate the conflict, change, and uniqueness in the daily activities of government.

A totally different pattern from the one described above may often exist, and it is difficult to say which pattern is more prevalent. Reporters and government officials may often develop a symbiotic relationship, where the reporter does not dig too deeply and thus possibly embarrass the government official and, in return, is given enough material to keep his employer happy. One journalist claims that this is perhaps the biggest danger that reporters face.[7] Certainly, the reporter who acts as a "stooge" does not have any weight in the policy-making process.

Policy Development

The reporter is in several ways a participant in policy development. First, he can stimulate activity on the part of government officials, thus speeding up the decision-making process, simply by focusing attention on the matter. One study quotes a reporter as saying, "You can call someone up and ask him how something is coming along. He just can't say he is doing nothing. He *has* to say he is looking into it and will let you know in a few days."[8] Second, the reporter exacerbates conflict by giving it attention. Parties to a dispute may become further estranged when they read reports of critical remarks about them carried in the press. Third, as a scrutiny of stories shows, the reporter is a policy advocate. He may have strong convictions about the right kind of policy in certain areas, such as health or education, and thus may consciously or unconsciously bias his writing. Finally, the reporter can sometimes directly advocate policy, usually in columns and feature stories, as well as through personal advice to decision makers.[9] And, of course, editors present their views in the editorial pages.

Editorials, features, and columns are not the means by which the news media exercise the greatest amount of influence over the public and government officials. Rather, as a number of authors have pointed out, the essence of their power lies in their ability to set the agenda for public thinking and discussion. As one authority points out: "The press is significantly more than a purveyor of information and opinion. It may not be successful much of the time in telling people what to think, but it is stunningly successful in telling its readers what to think *about*."[10]

Evidence of newspapers' conscious attempts to set the agenda for public discussion can be seen most readily at the level of urban government, although it is also obvious at the state level. They crusade against drug addiction or vice, or campaign for a new civic center. An example of the extent to which the media can make people aware of developments is found in a case study of St. Louis politics that examined the defeat of a plan that would have created a single-district government for the city and county. Of the persons interviewed, 57 percent in the city and 74 percent in the county had heard of the plan through the leading St. Louis paper, while 57 percent in the city and 70 percent in the county had heard of the plan through the local television stations. However, only 28 percent of the city sample and 49 percent of the county sample could tell the position taken by the newspaper, which had vigorously worked on behalf of the plan. The impact of the media, then, lies more in the direction of agenda setting than actually influencing policy outcomes.[11]

Policy Implementation

Reportorial norms guarantee that the day-to-day functioning of the bureaucracy at any level of government will not be covered. Although state capital newspapers publish reams of copy about the deliberations of the state legislature when it is in session, one will search in vain for comparable coverage of agency programs. The same situation is even more characteristic of the urban level. The daily work of the bureaucrat may be of great importance, but it is unlikely to be characterized by spectacular conflict, change, uniqueness, or names. In addition, it is increasingly highly complex, so that the reporter's task of explanation becomes correspondingly more difficult. Further, since agencies are specialized, only a small part of the readership is greatly concerned with the functioning of any particular bureau.[12] Persons without a relative or friend in a city hospital, for example, are unlikely to be greatly concerned about such institutions.

Bureaucrats are less likely than other political actors to be influenced by the press. First, bureaucrats are not so prone to develop close ties with reporters as are elected officials, because the reporter's definition of what is news causes him to focus on the elected official. Second, as pointed out earlier, bureaucrats may often enjoy a good deal of autonomy in carrying out a program and may therefore not need press support. When such is not the case, they may seek to cultivate the press.[13]

One relatively recent type of journalistic entry into policy implementation is the trouble-shooting role played by some media in response to reader complaints. Newspapers and television and radio stations have columns or shows to which people complain about allegedly unfair treatment by public or private agencies. In many cases, the media have been able to force an agency to change its actions. This kind of intervention fills the gap created by the demise of or decline in saliency of the party official in some areas, and it may have a substantial cumulative impact.

The generalizations advanced here are quite broad and certainly do not pretend to explain the complex web of relationships between reporters and bureaucrats. For example, are bureaus that assert themselves aggressively and that wish to expand rapidly more dependent upon the press than bureaus content with the status quo, and do they seek more to influence it? Are bureaus that are not highly professionalized and within the chief executive's chain of command more likely to be influenced by press reporting than highly professionalized, structurally autonomous bureaus? While common sense might lead to a tentative "yes" to both questions and to other similar ones, firm answers are impossible until more studies of bureau-media interaction are completed.

ADVISORY GROUPS AND CONSULTANTS

Another category of actors is those who provide information and advice to other actors. As society and government become more complex, the advisory function becomes more and more important. He who has the ear of government officials may wield great influence.

Policy Development

The *task force* is utilized with increasing frequency by state and urban chief executives, following the president's lead, and is set up to provide the executive with information and policy recommendations in areas where he wants a fresh perspective (by-passing the bureaucracy) or perhaps wishes to avoid the pain of making a decision all by himself. Typically, a task force is a "blue-ribbon" committee, with leaders of different elites as members; the business community is usually especially well represented. Task force groups meet with mixed success, for there is no guarantee that either the governor or legislature will support their proposals. In fact, the true purpose behind some of them seems to be a desire to satisfy interest group demand that a problem be confronted. Once the task force has finished its work, its proposals may be ignored because no important political actors had any intention in the first place of seriously considering its work. The task force is, though, at the very least, a potential means for the executive to reduce his reliance on the line bureaucracy for information.

The *think tanks*, research corporations that arose in the post-World War II period and that derive most of their contracts from the Defense Department,[14] can be either profit or nonprofit corporations. General Electric's TEMPO is representative of the former; the Hudson Institute, of the latter. In recent years an increasing number of think tanks have turned their attention to domestic policy. The RAND Corporation, in particular, has done a great deal of consulting for New York City since John Lindsay was elected mayor in 1965, studying such problems as fire and police department technology, and city health and housing programs. The Urban Institute in Washington, funded by the federal government, focuses solely on urban problems.[15] State agencies also contract with think tanks, in the fashion of the Vermont Public Service Board, which hired Overview, Inc., to study ways to run electric power lines.[16]

While it is difficult to argue that think tanks have had a significant effect on city and state policy making, their potential influence seems vast, if one considers their impact on national security policy.[17] Although think tanks have worked on problems since the end of World War II, they have only recently entered the area of domestic policy, and they are increasingly in evidence. By the year 2000, think tanks may be as powerful as any actor.

More specialized *substantive issue consultants,* such as engineering and planning firms, are frequently engaged by governments, though typically for work of a less generalized nature than that of the think tanks. Bureaus may employ this type of consultant, as well as the think tank, for tactical purposes, to add weight to their arguments that certain policies should be followed.[18] Chief executives, again, will be motivated to employ the think tank and other consultants as a means of gaining information from a source other than the bureaucracy.

As already noted, many agencies have an *advisory board*, or committee. In some cases such a body does far more than provide information or policy recommendations, since it may have authority to approve certain proposed programs before they can go into effect. The impetus for the establishment of an advisory board usually comes from either the bureau or its interest group clientele; the former favors such a board when it feels that a board will provide it with a means to better influence its clientele, the latter when it wants easier access to the agency. The occupational make-up of an advisory board's membership provides an excellent clue to the nature of an agency's most important clientele groups, regardless of who was responsible for establishing the board in the first place. The advisory board seems, for the most part, to be the monopoly of a bureau and its clientele, not a structure created by and responsive to other actors.

Policy Implementation

The advisory board is likely to play as important a role in policy implementation as in policy development; the think tanks and the specialized substantive policy consultants, at this juncture, are much less likely to do so; and the task force is unlikely to become involved to any extent in policy implementation. Other groups exist that are more likely to become involved in policy implementation than policy development. As the Council of State Governments has argued, "Most state agencies . . . find it necessary to seek outside help in solving their organization, management, or technical problems."[19]   Observations of state government officials such as that of Illinois Director of General Services John A. Kennedy are typical: "There is a continuing need for the employment of outside consultants in many professional areas of state government."[20]   There are now two principal types of management consultants, although think tanks such as New York RAND are involving themselves increasingly in this area.

There have been *institutes* associated with universities and/or the reform movement since the turn of the century, though many were founded later. They are nonprofit corporations whose income is derived from contracts and, in some cases, endowments or public funds. Leading examples today include the Institute of Public Administration in New York City and the Public Administration Service. The institutes focus, for the most part, on managerial and organizational analyses, advising governments how to set up a personnel department or organize an accounting system. In some states, such as Michigan, Georgia, North Carolina, and California, university bureaus of government research seem to be especially important government management consultants.[21]

Private corporations as well as government agencies are among the clients of *profit-making management consultants.*   McKinsey and Co., Inc., and Booz, Allen, and Hamilton, Inc., are two preeminent firms in the field. A smaller company that has conducted studies of the entire executive branch of more than ten states for their governors is Warren King and Associates of Chicago. In the wake of these studies, substantial changes have been made in the organization and technical management of many bureaus.

The most striking change in the advisory area since World War II has been the rise of the outside consultant. This development is so new that it is not surprising how little is known about the relative impact of the different types in different settings. Unlike the case of some other actors examined so far, however, it seems safe to predict that there will soon be a good deal more knowledge about these outside experts in a society that has become increasingly concerned with the implications of the current wave of specialized and scientific knowledge.[22]

Conclusion

Communications media and advisory groups play differing roles in bureaucratic politics. The former may be either supportive or antagonistic regarding bureau policies, but whatever role they may play, they are unlikely to have great impact on bureaucrats. The latter, of which there are many different types, already have substantial influence over bureaucratic policy making, and this influence is growing.

CHAPTER SEVEN

Intergovernmental Relations

Another set of actors of tremendous importance to city and state governments are federal government agencies. In addition, there is a great deal of interaction between city and state agencies, so an inspection of the workings of the federal system is a necessary step for better understanding of the political life of state and city agencies.

STATE-CITY RELATIONS: CITY POLICY DEVELOPMENT

Until recently, New Mexico cities were unable to operate their own bus systems and discontinue water service to customers who had not paid their bills.[1] New state laws had to be passed before the cities could act in these areas. New Mexico is not an exception to the general rule: legally and constitutionally, city governments are creatures of the state and are regulated by a host of state agencies. City government charters are granted by the state legislature, which can change city boundaries, delimit their taxing powers and debt liabilities, and tell them how they must run their schools. In addition, grants of authority by the state to urban governments are construed in a very narrow way. If the courts find that there is any doubt about a city government's having jurisdiction in a certain area, such as health, they will deny jurisdiction to the city.[2]

Some half of the states have *home-rule* provisions in their constitutions, which enable a city to act on its own in designated matters, such as law enforcement and public health, without first going to the legislature. However, home rule is not the panacea that its proponents, who wished to increase urban authority, had hoped it would be, because city autonomy under home rule is restricted to the designated areas, and even there the state can intervene in many cases. State legislation is paramount over local legislation; a state agency can force a local government to accede to state law, even when the local government has an agency and legislation of its own under which to work. For example, New York City—a home-rule city—is required by the state to appropriate for its schools a fixed percentage of the assessed valuation of taxable property. The state also directs the city to include policemen and firemen in the competitive class of civil service and to rotate their shifts and vacation schedules.[3] In addition, a state can require that city proposals and actions be approved by the state before they can take effect, and that the state review city agency actions.

While city governments operate at a constitutional disadvantage vis-à-vis state governments, they have substantial resources to influence the states. Because cities are part of the state political system, send representatives to the legislature, are important in the constituency of statewide-elected officials, and furnish party leaders, they have a profound impact on state policy. Furthermore, interest groups within the cities have close bonds with kindred groups in the state, and together they are a strong force in shaping policies that relate specifically to the cities.[4] Finally, and most relevant to this discussion, city agencies are among the major clientele groups of many state agencies. State police, welfare, and education departments must work closely with their local counterparts if they are to operate effectively.

There are certainly great variations, both by region and area, in the extent of state influence over local agencies. The Hawaii State Department of Education, for example, directly runs all public schools, while public education is primarily a local government function in the rest of the country. It seems that city welfare departments have less power relative to their state counterparts than do city departments of education. Certainly variations in school policy among cities in the same state are more visible than variations in welfare policy.

The effectiveness of local government demands on state government is reflected in the financial relationships between the two entities. In fiscal year 1969, from their total budgets of $74.2 billion, the state governments transferred $24.8 billion to the localities in grants-in-aid, an amount that accounted for 30 percent of the latter's total budget of $81.9 billion. By far the greatest share of this money, some $15 billion, was for education, while highways and welfare absorbed $6.5 billion. Research on managers of American cities over 100,000 population indicates their awareness of the importance of state money; most of their time spent in intergovernmental relations was with state officials in charge of highways and education.[5] Cities are literally dependent upon state grants-in-aid for their survival, whether they like it or not. And many city officials do not like it, because they believe that state governments have been unresponsive to their problems.[6] Recent surveys show that city officials think the federal government is more helpful than state government in urban problem solving.[7]

STATE-CITY RELATIONS: CITY POLICY IMPLEMENTATION

There is wide variety in the power relationships between city and state agencies in city policy implementation. In some cases, state agencies lead their city government clientele; in other cases, they act as partners; and in still others, they may be captives.[8] Generally speaking, highly professionalized city agencies are more likely than less professionalized agencies to exert influence on their state counterparts. Local health and hospital departments probably carry more weight with their state counterparts than do generalist city officials with state departments of urban affairs. City agencies that share relatively little activity with, or receive relatively little financial aid from, such state equivalents as public works or parks departments neither wield much influence nor are subject to it vis-à-vis the state agency.

State agencies have less effect in city policy implementation than in policy development, because they do not have the manpower to supervise city agencies. City agencies are much larger in the aggregate than state agencies, because they directly implement programs on a "street-level" basis every day. Until state agencies do nothing else but regulate city agency policy implementation, their role in policy implementation must of necessity be less than that of city government.

FEDERAL RELATIONS WITH CITIES AND STATES: POLICY DEVELOPMENT

The three levels of government in the United States are not equal in legal authority. Federal laws in conflict with state and city laws supersede the latter, unless federal law conflicts with the federal constitution itself. At the same time, states and cities have great discretion in legislating, as evidenced by the differences among state and city welfare laws. Welfare benefits and regulations concerning the work status and private behavior of recipients vary tremendously. Further, states enjoy much greater legal authority as compared with the federal government than do cities in relation to state governments. The federal constitution created the federal government but not the state governments, which already existed; and the constitution gives the states a number of guarantees against federal intrusion. These include prohibition against tampering with state borders and the provision that each state shall have two federal senators. The Constitution is largely what the federal courts interpret it to be, and over the years they have made it clear that the national government cannot impose on the states controls such as debt limits or prescribe administrative agency forms. The states, however, can and do impose such controls on city governments.

Two Models of Intergovernmental Relations

Perhaps the most widely held view of the nature of the relationship between federal agencies and state and local agencies is the conflict model, according to which the normal relationship between these levels is characterized by antagonism and tension. The "feds" try to foist programs on state and city agencies who resist as best they can and try to go their own way. Many people with this perspective believe that the federal government is increasingly encroaching on the prerogatives of city and state government, to the point where a federal takeover will occur in the not too distant future.

There is no question that conflict abounds, not only between federal officials and city and state officials, but between city and state officials. There is a good chance that any issue of a daily newspaper will report a contest. City and state bureaucrats frequently accuse the "feds" of being unresponsive, arbitrary, and slow in their decision making on joint programs. Federal officials, on the other hand, feel that local officials often try to evade the letter or spirit of the laws covering joint programs. Although the conflict model certainly contains elements of reality, it is oversimplified.

Morton Grodzins and his students have described the federal system as one characterized by "sharing" and cooperation rather than conflict or growing federal domination. They argue that when conflict does occur, it is more likely to be among actors in one level of government than among actors in different levels. For example, state legislators are much more likely to contend with the state chief executive and state bureaucrats rather than to ally with them against the federal government.[10]

One can quarrel with Grodzins's interpretation and argue that it gives insufficient weight to conflict in the federal system. In recent years, for instance, associations of city and state government chief executives have inveighed against the federal government. To illustrate, in the middle 1960s the Council of State Governments published "Federal Grant-in-Aid Requirements Impeding State Administration" and "Cost to the States Resulting from Delays in Authorization or Appropriation of Federal Grants-in-Aid."[11] Officials of the United States Conference of Mayors and the National League of Cities have also voiced displeasure over federal regulations and guidelines. However, Grodzins has delineated in great detail the enormous amount of "sharing" in the federal system. The term "sharing" describes situations where decision making is carried out jointly by the three levels of government, or where officials of all three have important responsibility in administration, or where all three are influential in operation of a given program.[12] As Grodzins points out, "A root fact of sharing is the nature of American law. In virtually no field does the complete body of law with respect to a given governmental activity have its source in one of these so-called levels of government. In a typical case a mixture of federal, state, and local regulation covers an area of regulation or activity."[13] Grodzins's treatment of federal regulatory agencies, for example, shows how they have become very closely linked with their state equivalents. The Transportation Act of 1920, which is typical of regulatory legislation, required the Interstate Commerce Commission to notify state regulatory commissions when any business before it related to their activities.[14] Grodzins's contention that there is almost no area of government concern that is not shared is supported by instances of state and local government activity in foreign policy, which most persons would no doubt assume to be the sole province of the federal government. Today the state of Florida continues to seize Cuban fishing boats in its waters, rather than calling in federal officials, while California has continuing arguments with Mexico about water usage. Even the regulation of atomic energy is a shared function, with the states being allowed jurisdiction over most uses of atomic energy within their borders.[15]

Grodzins and his students have stressed the capacity of urban and state governments to affect the intergovernmental process through contacts with congressmen and interest groups. For example, a congressman can be influenced by a state agency from his home state, because the agency is the only source of expertise that is attuned to local needs. Although he can secure information from federal agencies, they may not be so understanding of local conditions as a state agency. In addition, the state agency may service constituents' complaints for the congressman, making it likely he will return the favor by helping the agency in its negotiations with the federal government. Also, as discussed in more detail below, the state agency can use national associations of state agencies as a lobby or pressure group in its effort to get what it wants in the national arena.[16]

Federal Grants-in-Aid

Perhaps the best way to appreciate the effects of the federal system on the politics of urban and state bureaucracy is to examine the nature of the federal grants-in-aid, because of the impact they have on urban and state governments. As a number of writers have noted, the federal government has become a crucial source of revenue for urban and state governments.[17] Most federal revenue is raised through the income tax, which yields new revenue commensurate with economic expansion. In contrast, the states and cities raise the bulk of their money through sales and property taxes, which do not yield increased revenue at such a rapid rate. While most of the states and some cities have income taxes, these taxes are usually not constructed to yield very large sums of money or to grow with economic expansion. The states and cities could design new tax structures similar to the federal income tax, but such a course is so politically unpopular that they have not done so. Increasingly, then, local officials look to Washington for money.[18] Astute city and state officials are aware of the potential largesse to be gained from the "feds," and work diligently for it.[19] Urban politicians, in fact, long ago gave up on the state governments as primary revenue sources for new programs, and they now concentrate their efforts on the federal government.[20]

In the 1960s, for example, there was a flood of new federal-aid programs in such areas as antipoverty, model cities, public housing, and education of low-income children. While some states did innovate by creating departments of urban affairs and expanding spending in a number of fields, state innovation did not match the federal effort. Most state governments have not been sympathetic to the problems of the cities, first, because state legislatures were malapportioned to overrepresent rural interests, and, second, although the federal courts ended this imbalance, the bulk of the population has moved from the central cities to the suburbs.

Although cities and states still raise most of their own revenue, the federal contribution to the totals is rising, as Table 1 illustrates. Tables 2 and 3 indicate the relationships among levels of government in raising and spending revenues.[21] Note that while local government raises the smallest amount of revenue, it *spends* a good deal more as a result of transfers from the state and federal governments. In fact, local government spends more on *domestic* programs (programs other than defense, international affairs, and space) than either the state or federal level.

There are a number of different types of federal grants. Federal aid is conditional in nature—certain "strings" are attached. Although all aid has strings, the strings differ. One way of classifying aid is by the extent to which a unit of government must match funds, or contribute its own money. With this yardstick, three types of grant-in-aid can be distinguished. First, there are *flat grants*, which are fixed sums, regardless of

TABLE 1.
Federal-Aid Outlays in Relation to Total Federal Outlays and to State-Local Revenue

| Fiscal Year | Federal Aid | | | |
	Amount (millions)	As % of Total Federal Outlays	As % of Domestic Federal Outlays*	As % of State-Local Revenue†
1959	$ 6,669	7.2	15.9	12.3
1960	7,040	7.6	16.4	11.6
1961	7,112	7.3	15.4	11.0
1962	7,893	7.4	15.8	11.3
1963	8,634	7.8	16.5	11.6
1964	10,141	8.6	17.9	12.4
1965	10,904	9.2	18.4	12.4
1966	12,960	9.7	19.2	13.2
1967	15,240	9.6	19.5	14.2
1968	18,599	10.4	20.9	15.8
1969	20,255	11.0	21.3	15.3
1970	23,954	12.2	21.9	15.9
1971	29,844	14.1	23.5	17.9
1972 (estimate)	39,080	16.5	25.8	21.1
1973 (estimate)	43,479	17.6	27.0	21.1

Source: *Special Analyses, Budget of the U.S. Government, Fiscal Year 1973*, p. 245.
*Excluding outlays for defense, space, and international programs.
†Bureau of the Census, *Governmental Finances in 1969-70.*

TABLE 2.

Revenue Raised and Spent by Each Level of Government,
Fiscal Year 1969, in Percent
(Total Revenue: $312.6 Billion; Total Domestic Spending: $188 Billion)

	Federal	State	Local	Total
Money raised, by level of government	63.9	19.1	17.0	100
Money spent, by level of government	57.7	17.1	25.1	100
Money spent, by level of government, on domestic programs	30.3	28.2	41.5	100

TABLE 3.

Intergovernmental Revenue Transfers, Fiscal Year 1969,
in Billions of Dollars

Federal Aid to States	Federal Aid to Localities	State Aid to Localities	Local Aid to States
16.907	2.245	23.837	.867

conditions. They do not require formal matching by the recipient government, although in some cases the recipient must bear the administrative
costs of a program. Most of the federal land grants fell into this category.
Second, there are *proportionate grants*, which take into consideration the
contribution of a recipient government to a program, frequently on the
basis of a formula incorporating its needs and capabilities. Education
grants are usually of this type. Third, there are *percentage grants*, which
are allocated like proportionate grants, with the recipient government's
contribution a fixed percentage of the cost for maintaining a program.
Welfare grants are an example of this category.[22]

There are other restrictions besides the stipulation that the recipient
government must contribute funds to a program. Another way of looking
at federal grants-in-aid may give a somewhat clearer idea of the nature of
the strings attached.[23] First, *project grants* are those which require project-
by-project federal approval of applications from the state or local governments, and they are generally made for a specified time period. Thus,
project grants give a very broad degree of control to the federal agency,
since it can review individual projects. Examples include the urban renewal,
public housing, and Model Cities programs. Second, *formula grants* provide
funds to agencies without their having made application, as long as the
agencies match funds and follow federal guidelines in using the funds.
These grants are made according to a formula established by Congress or
the administration that is based on fixed-objective criteria, such as population or area. The flow of funds is continuous, and the decisions on each

project are left to the recipient agency. Examples include welfare and many education programs. Most federal grants are project grants, a trend that became more evident in the 1960s. In 1962 there were some 160 grant-in-aid programs, of which about 50 were formula grants, and 110 project grants. By 1969, however, there were over 460 federal grant-in-aid programs, of which some 80 were formula grants, and the remaining 380-odd were project grants; in dollar amounts, however, the totals for both types were roughly equal.[24] Aid to cities has been project-oriented, while state aid has been for broader programs.[25]

Finally, yet another classification distinguishes among grants by the scope of the programs involved. While *categorical grants* are for narrowly circumscribed projects such as special training programs for the physically handicapped, *block grants* are for a broad policy area, with no restrictions except that they be spent in a particular policy area. Block grants finance a broad function and thus give the recipient government a good deal of discretion. Recent examples include the 1966 consolidation of sixteen individual health grants and the 1967 juvenile delinquency prevention and control act.

The impact of federal grants on city and state government programs has been enormous, because the subnational units tend to go where the money is.[26] Federal money shapes the direction of urban and state government policy development in both subtle and direct ways. Surveys of state government executives, for example, indicate that half of them would spend federal grant money in ways other than conditions of the grant dictate.[27] An analysis of grants allotted in 1960 showed that the federal dollar stimulated ninety-four cents in state and local government spending; fifty cents was mandated by matching requirements, but the other forty-four cents was over and above the requirement.[28] Federal grants, then, stimulate additional state and local spending far in excess of the matching requirement. In addition, once an agency agrees to accept federal funds, it must meet federal standards, thus constraining its role in future program development. For example, when a city agency says that it will meet federal water standards in return for aid, it will find it very difficult, if not impossible, to subsequently abandon the standards, whether or not aid continues. It not only has made a commitment to the federal government, but has begun programs that will attract clientele who insist that previous standards be maintained.

Federal aid also requires that recipients conform with federal laws and practices that previously may have had no impact on the area. For instance, if they are to continue to receive aid, public and private institutions of higher education must consent to formulate plans for the hiring of minorities and women as professional staff members.

The federal system is not a one-way influence flow system. States and cities can refuse federal aid, or their congressmen or interest groups can lobby federal agencies for exceptions and changes. For example, there are always states in violation of requirements for welfare aid, but they never have grants withheld. Instead, bargaining among federal bureaucrats, state bureaucrats, congressmen, and other relevant political actors brings about some kind of compromise.

Just as is the case in state-city government interaction, the stand and strength of federal bureau clientele groups is a good indication of whether the bureau will prevail or have to retreat when it is on a collision course with state and city agencies. It is not much of a surprise to see federal welfare officials back off from conflicts with states. The Army Corps of Engineers, because of strong support from the U.S. Public Works Association, the National Rivers and Harbors Congress, and local businessmen and contractors, rarely needs to modify its proposals for public works at the behest of local officials.

It is difficult to go beyond such broad generalizations at this point in time. Interest in intergovernmental relations is increasing, and more elaborate typologies, based on an adequate number of studies, should soon be available.

FEDERAL RELATIONS WITH CITIES AND STATES: POLICY IMPLEMENTATION

Besides their effects in program terms, federal grants have altered the nature of state and city policy implementation. First, they have significantly enlarged state and urban civil service coverage. Many federal agencies set as a condition for grants-in-aid that the recipient agency have a merit system. This stipulation has been typical in the areas of health, education, and welfare, and although it is difficult to ascertain the exact figures, civil service coverage has been extended to thousands of positions. Thus, in helping to accelerate the steady but slow growth of civil service in the states and cities, federal grant-in-aid policy has restricted the influence of party organization leaders in this area. Other related management practices, such as federal auditing, are increasingly being required.

Second, federal intervention has limited local agency administrative discretion. Within specific policy areas, federal grants have contributed to much more uniformity in programs and administrative procedures. Federal standards are often very detailed, so that much less leeway than would otherwise be the case remains for agencies, whether they are implementing educational, solid-waste disposal, or health care programs.

City and state agencies that are determined to evade federal direction can do so to a great extent. A recent study of the impact of federal grants on the management of state departments of education found differential responses to the grant conditions by recipients. Some were content to follow in the policy direction set by the U.S. Office of Education by changing their department orientation. Others, however, simply created new bureaus and staff to comply with the federal regulations and did not change their policy orientation whatsoever.[29]

The third and most important influence of federal grants on state and city governments has been the imposition of the *single-state agency* requirement, in effect since the beginning of the century. Regardless of where federal grants end up, they are typically administered through a state agency. When Congress designates a single-state agency to administer a grant program, it does not usually grant the chief executive (governor or mayor) a voice in the policy-making process involving the grant. Federal laws require a single-state agency to administer grants in areas as diverse as highways, infant care, urban planning, civil defense, and water pollution control. The consequences of this requirement are enormous, because they fortify the tendency of urban and state administrative agencies, as well as their federal counterparts, to autonomy. The agencies themselves could not design a more ideal requirement, since it prevents the chief executive and legislature from "meddling" in the agency's administration of grants. The federal requirement has in this way reinforced the built-in disposition of urban and state governments toward fragmentation of policy, since there is no requirement or incentive for an agency to cooperate with functionally related agencies in policy making. For example, it is possible today for a locality to apply to several federal agencies for aid in planning the construction of water and sewer facilities. In a given state, funds from five federal agencies are, in all likelihood, administered by five different state agencies.

The single-state agency requirement, as can easily be imagined, has long been the despair of chief executives. Not only are they unable to coordinate federal grants, but they are often prevented by the requirement from reorganizing their own executive branch, even when they have the full support of the legislature. A reorganization plan in one state sought to shift the Bureau of Sight Conservation from the Division of Vocational Rehabilitation to the Department of Social Services to bring together the two closely related functions. However, the bureau could not be transferred because of Section 401.1 (29 U.S.C. 35), which restricted the organizational placement of such a program to a "state agency primarily concerned with vocational rehabilitation."[30] Likewise, the Department of Health, Education, and Welfare prevented the state of Oregon from setting up a state-equivalent of HEW; reorganization plans for California, Hawaii, and Wisconsin were vetoed for the same reason.[31]

Another consequence of the single-state agency requirement is extremely narrow program categories, which results in nonfunctional restrictions. Examples include the heart fund public health nurse who is not supposed to help cancer and TB patients, even when they are in a household she is visiting; forced separation of mental health and mental retardation projects; and restriction on the transfer of unused federal funds from one district to another where they could be utilized.[32]

How can the single-state agency requirement be explained?   While it was originally devised to make sure that one agency would be responsible and thus accountable for grant programs, today it is sustained by the power of what Harold Seidman has called "largely self-governing professional guilds," or associations of professional urban and state government officials.[33]   One such guild is the American Vocational Association, which has been able to torpedo attempts by presidents to break its hold on vocational training, first established in the Smith-Hughes Act of 1917.   Other like groups are the Council of Chief State School Officers, the National Education Association, and the American Association of State Highway Officers.   Their membership includes the program administrators of the line agencies themselves, who view chief executives and top management generalists "as potential or actual enemies, subject to the fluctuating whims of the electorate."[34]   Frequently, the bureau chief of the federal agency has previously headed a state agency and is a member of the professional association.   Professional ties among these administrators at whatever level are very strong and go a long way toward explaining why the single-state agency requirement persists.

Guild influence is sustained by the "policy triangle": the federal agency; the congressional subcommittee, which has jurisdiction over the agency; and the interest group clientele of the agency, which is often no other than the self-governing guilds, making up at least a very large part of the agency's clientele.   Given this kind of power configuration, it is no surprise that the single-state agency requirement exists in the grant-in-aid system and continues to flourish, in spite of the discontent of other actors in the system and recent challenges to it.   One such challenge is the Intergovernmental Cooperation Act of 1968, which authorized the waiver of the single-state agency requirement in certain cases and directed that the chief executive and the legislature be informed of all grants to state agencies, that aid be consistent with the objectives of state, regional, and local planning, and that loans and grants be made to units of general local government rather than to agencies concerned with only specific policies.   To date, there has been little gubernatorial use of the waiver, presumably due to both lack of interest on the part of governors and their knowledge that such action would precipitate vehement conflict with the guilds.

REVENUE SHARING

In 1972 Congress approved general revenue sharing, a program that allots several billion dollars per year to the states and cities, with very few strings attached.   The act was the result of pressure by a broad coalition of city and state officials, especially chief executives and their aides, and

represented their response to the politico-fiscal crisis of subnational government. President Nixon supported general revenue sharing and has also
pushed for what he calls special revenue sharing: a great expansion in
block grants through the consolidation of billions of dollars in categorical
grant programs, such as transportation and education. The president has
also requested authority to initiate additional consolidation of categorical
programs into block grants when he thinks it appropriate in the future,
unless such proposals are vetoed by Congress within sixty days. If adopted
and implemented in an aggressive fashion by chief executives, the proposals
would end the single-state agency mode of carrying on federal grant business. However, even if special revenue sharing were to be enacted by
Congress, it is unclear just what such a program would do to the present
balance of power in the federal system between the guilds and the chief
executives.

Because there are some areas in which block grants already exist, some
conclusions can be made about the likely adoption of such a plan. The
record is not one to provide supporters of the president's reform proposals
a sanguine outlook on the efficacy of special revenue sharing as a means
for promoting program goals, or drastically reducing guild power. One
illustration is the Partnership for Health Act of 1966, a precursor of the
Intergovernmental Cooperation Act, which offered to governors the prospect of an increased role in health policy making. The Secretary of Health,
Education, and Welfare asked them to decide which would be the single-
state agency. Sixteen governors designated an agency that was under gubernatorial control, such as a planning agency, or the central administration of
finance agency, or even the governor's office itself. However, the act has
failed to relate policy in this health program closely to the state chief
executives. Over two-thirds of the single-state agencies are not organizationally close to the governor. A study of the implementation of the
program concludes that "the majority of the comprehensive health planning agencies have not been closely related to their states' chief executives
. . . only seven of the forty-eight agencies for which materials were available
described what could be called a close working relationship with the
governor."[35]

Perhaps the best-known block grant is the 1968 Omnibus Crime Control and Safe Streets Act, which supplies funds for law enforcement assistance to the states and localities through the Law Enforcement Assistance
Administration (LEAA). Although the money goes through the governor
and thus avoids the single-state agency requirement, the program has met
with one problem after another. In many cases, state governments have
shown no great interest in making sure that the funds filter down to the
metropolitan areas needing them most, since that is where the crime rate is
growing most rapidly. The United States Conference of Mayors has argued
that

though the legislative history in surrounding enactment of the Safe Streets Act, and language in the statute itself, clearly intended for LEAA to provide support for projects developed at the local level, the discretionary program is increasingly being used by LEAA to impose its "impact" priorities on the cities. . . . Miami, Florida, and Birmingham, Alabama, for example, have received almost no funds under the Safe Streets Act from their states. . . . Major cities in the states of Alabama, Arizona, Indiana, Nebraska, Florida, Virginia, and others are not even receiving a share of funds that approximates their share of the state population. More to the point, very few cities with major crime problems in this country are receiving a share of funds which approximates their share of the state's crime rate.[36]

As Henry Ruth, director of the New York City Criminal Justice Coordinating Council, the city's designated planning group for funds available from LEAA, stated:

We have to go to three separate boards for approval of every project. We have over 170 processing steps before funding comes. In addition to the three boards, in every project we have to go through the city comptroller, the state comptroller, the city corporation counsel, the state attorney general, the city budget bureau, and the personnel bureau. There are civil service problems in some grants. I do not think there is an agency in New York we haven't gotten to know intimately in seventeen months, just in processing grants at either the city or state level. That leaves out all the federal problems with discretionary grants. . . . I have been in meetings the National League of Cities has sponsored with the thirty largest cities, and I hear some terrible tales of people in cities that have no idea how much money is coming from the state. I do not know how you can plan on that basis. How can you set out a plan if you have no idea how much money you are going to get?[37]

Thus, substituting block grants for categorical grants may not bring the new tomorrow foreseen by the advocates of grant consolidation. The quarrel over the type of grant-in-aid structure is a power struggle at all levels of government among chief executives and their allies who face opposition from the self-governing guilds in policy triangles. This struggle will certainly go on for a long time. Federal grants of whatever type will continue to be of growing importance to state and urban governments in the years ahead, and the struggle among advocates of different grant-in-aid systems will be a fascinating and increasingly visible one.

Conclusion

Relations among city, state, and federal governments constitute a highly complex web of power relationships, especially after the recent growth and changes in the federal grant-in-aid system. While grants-in-aid may increase the power of the donor over the recipient government in some cases, ours is truly an intergovernmental system, with substantial power remaining in city and state governments.

CHAPTER EIGHT

The Politics of Budgeting

In the preceding chapters, we have examined, one by one, the interaction of various actors with the bureaucracy. This approach provides much insight into policy making, but it necessarily oversimplifies by concentrating on the bureaucracy and only one other actor at a time, when in reality the bureaucracy interacts simultaneously with all these actors.

This chapter focuses on the budgetary process, enabling the reader to evaluate the interaction of several actors with the bureaucracy. While some agencies, like municipally owned electric power plants, need not submit requests for budgetary funds, because they are self-financing through user fees, most must look to the legislature for their financing. A few receive money for a two-year period; most have annual allocations, which means that budget politics never cease. The budget constitutes the action plan of an agency and is the means through which the agency outlines its program goals. The budget, then, is the concern of all actors in bureaucratic politics.

TYPES OF BUDGETARY SYSTEMS

There are different types of budgetary systems, most of which share the following characteristics. First, the initial and basic responsibility for preparation of the bureau's budget rests with the bureau itself. The chief officials, in conjunction with the budget officers, draw up a list of items—salaries, equipment, services, and the like—and their projected costs for the next fiscal period. Second, this information is reviewed by the central budget office, which submits it along with its suggestions to the chief executive. Third, the chief executive, after studying all the materials sent to him, makes his budget recommendations to the legislature. Fourth, the legislature appropriates money for the agency as it sees fit, for it is not usually bound by the recommendations it receives. Fifth, the funds go to the central budget office, which allots them to the agencies. Finally, the agencies themselves spend the funds.

It was not until the twentieth century that the chief executive in both state and city governments came to center stage in the budgetary process. Before then, the legislature dealt directly with executive agencies, giving each its appropriation. No central budget office existed, nor did the chief executive submit recommendations to the legislature. The only form of postappropriation control was through the auditor, whose job it was to make sure no money had been spent illegally.[1]

The same reformers who supported the manager form of government and nonpartisan elections backed the creation of an executive budget system, in which the chief executive would review and revise agency budget requests before they were submitted to the legislature, and supervise spending after the legislature had appropriated funds. The thrust of the executive budget movement was the desire to give the chief executive greater control over spending, and thus to increase coordination and reduce waste. The executive budget, like budgets in use before it, focused on the objects of expenditure, or the items that were to be acquired by the agency —personnel, supplies, equipment. Since each line in the budget lists different items, it is known as a *line-item budget.* Today this kind of budget is the most common American budgetary form. There are still, however, a number of governmental jurisdictions in which the chief executive must share his authority to prepare the budget and supervise agency spending with other executive agencies that are largely beyond his control. Such is the case in weak-mayor government, where the mayor may be required to share budgetary power with an appointed career civil servant or a finance board or committee, as well as for a minority of governors.

Another type of budgetary system is *performance budgeting,* which was originated in 1914 by the New York Bureau of Municipal Research. The emphasis of performance budgeting is not on objects of expenditure, but on functions such as health and welfare activities and projects; its proponents believe that this leads to more rational budgetary allocations. Per-unit cost of such government activities as hospital operation is often calculated under performance systems in an attempt at more meaningful evaluation. A number of state governments have adopted performance budgeting, but one researcher discovered that most use only some of its techniques; only seven states adopted all four techniques—the inclusion of narrative information in the budget, the use of activity classifications, the collection and publication of workload data, and the use of cost statistics— that he felt were characteristic of the system.[3]

City governments have been more enthusiastic about performance budgeting, though no precise figures on its extent have been gathered. City managers, in particular, have advocated performance budgeting, because they believe it leads to more rational program evaluation. In spite of its use in a number of areas, it is difficult to conclude that adoption of performance budgeting as such leads to basic changes in budgetary decision making, a theme explored later.

The newest type of budgetary system is the *Planning-Programming-Budgeting System* (PPBS) which differs from performance budgeting in several ways. First, rather than looking no further than one or two years into the future, PPBS projects expenditures over several years. While the budgetary process is usually an annual ritual, adherents of PPBS argue that the sensible way to plan programs is over a longer period of time. Second, where performance budgeting focuses on the functions and activities of government, PPBS focuses more squarely on the outputs of programs, to try to determine exactly what the programs accomplish. PPBS attempts to evaluate the costs and benefits of alternative programs in order to decide rationally which is the most valuable. For example, in the field of health, a performance budget breaks down departmental activities on a functional basis, listing such things as doctor licensing and hospital operation. PPBS looks instead at the actual results of departmental activities, in an effort to discern the impact on physical well-being that would result from different programs, so that decision makers will be in a better position to make allocations.[4]

PPBS is too new an arrival on the budgetary scene for its impact to be adequately assessed. It was first implemented in the early 1960s under Secretary of Defense Robert McNamara. While President Johnson ordered it to be implemented in all federal bureaus in 1965, it was implemented in form only, not in function.[5] It may exist on paper in a number of government jurisdictions, but in mid-1970, PPBS was not fully operative in a single state.[6] And though there are a number of cities, including New York and Philadelphia, that have made major moves to fully implement PPBS, there is no indication yet that budgetary decisions are made in ways other than those in which they were previously made.

One authority, Allen Schick, holds that each of the three budgetary systems is characterized by a different predominant function, although all share the other two functions as well. The chief function or emphasis of the line-item budget is *control,* or the enforcement of conditions and limitations set in the budget, and compliance with restrictions on expenditure. The primary task of the central budget agency is to make sure that line agencies observe the limitations and restrictions. The chief function of performance budgeting is *management,* or the attempt to achieve the most efficient use of resources in the implementation of authorized activities. The emphasis of PPBS is *planning,* or the determination of goals and evaluation of different programs designed to achieve the goals.[7]

Given these several emphases, it is not surprising that different political actors regard the various budgetary systems differentially. Performance budgeting and PPBS are usually backed by aides to the chief executive, who wish to see his place in the budgetary process enhanced. They believe that these two systems will enable him to evaluate more adequately the performance of agencies and to make more rational recommendations regarding the allocation each should receive. Mayors, managers, and governors are united with their budget offices in promoting PPBS.

Conversely, legislators and administrators of line agencies often oppose PPBS and favor retaining the line-item budget system. As noted in Chapter

3, legislators generally do not have a great amount of expertise in government programs, or sufficient staff to help them acquire such expertise. Thus, the functional focus of performance budgeting or PPBS usually bewilders them, because they are unable to appraise the program choices offered in these budgeting systems. They feel much more at home with a line-item budget, which enables them to make decisions to cut or add specific objects of expenditure, which are more concrete and which they feel better able to grasp.

The members of a legislative appropriations committee, furthermore, may see nothing but trouble in PPBS. These legislators usually have no great interest in specific programs, but rather in the total sum of appropriations. If they begin to make choices among programs, they will run into opposition from the leaders of substantive issue-area committees.

A minority of legislators actively support PPBS. As Robert Gilmour has pointed out, PPBS data would give legislators interested in making program choices information of much better quality.[8] Florida state legislators recently recognized this by adopting PPBS for state government. Their Hawaii counterparts are similarly oriented, constantly demanding more program information from the agencies so they can evaluate bureaucratic output.

Administrators of line agencies gain a number of advantages from the line-item budget that they feel are not available from the other budgeting systems. Schick notes that it enables them to manipulate facts and to claim supposed benefits for their programs. They invent staffing formulas and minimal standards, which are then compared to those of some other governmental jurisdiction that spends more, with the implicit argument that the budget decision makers should give the agency more. A system focusing on the functions or outputs of programs will not provide this kind of facade for administrators and may even indicate that they are not doing a very good job compared to other administrators. At present, the administrators of the line agencies hold the upper hand in determining whether PPBS will actually be implemented. Studies have shown that they are skilled at compiling a PPBS budget if they are directed to do so, but that there is no effective way in which overhead agencies can force them to accept the goals and rationale of PPBS.[9] Instead, the administrators can continue to focus on objects of expenditures, and if they have a close relationship with the legislature, they will continue to be funded. The only way for the chief executive and his overhead agencies to triumph is to see that the line agencies are staffed with supporters of PPBS and to persuade others, including legislators, to adopt a PPBS outlook.

PPBS does offer substantial benefits to line-agency bureaucrats who can master it. Educators have embraced PPBS in a time of declining enrollments and budgets, because its program emphasis may make boards and legislators think twice before eliminating or curtailing certain programs now, whereas cuts were previously measured only in objects of expenditure, like personnel or supplies. Some educators, indeed, have become so adept at manipulating data with PPBS that they can beat central budget office advocates of PPBS at their own game.[10]

While line-item budgeting continues to be the prevalent form in the United States, it seems that PPBS or systems akin to it are the wave of the future. Although PPBS has suffered setbacks at all levels of government after initial attempts to install it,[11] the usual response has been not to junk it, but to modify its scope, either by selecting certain agencies as PPBS analysis priorities or by not gathering as much information about agencies. Both New York and Massachusetts state governments, for example, have installed budgetary systems clearly modeled after PPBS, but the systems are not quite so ambitious and have other titles. While it may take decades for PPBS or its relatives to permeate governmental jurisdictions, PPBS seems likely to be as successful as other elements in the reform package, such as the manager form and nonpartisan elections. Schools of public administration are pushing PPBS today, as are graduate schools of education, which are training educational administrators. Thus, it is possible that the politics of budgetary systems will undergo a great deal of change. For the time being, however, almost all budgetary systems, whether performance or PPBS, are characterized by the political behavior, discussed below, that is associated with the line-item budget.

POLICY DEVELOPMENT: STATE BUDGETING

As is the case in any governmental jurisdiction, line-agency bureaucrats are the most important architects of budgets. Since they put together the proposals to which all the other actors react, bureaucrats are budgetary agenda-setters in a real sense. Because bureaucrats have more program information than the other actors, they use this resource both to draw up the budget document and to defend it. And they can have a great deal to say about exactly how this information is presented, as New York state bureaucrats proved in 1969 when they refused to comply any longer with PPBS regulations. Another key bureaucratic resource is the uncontrollability of the budget, brought about because the bulk of any governmental budget has been ordered under existing statutes and cannot be regulated by budgetary decision makers. The largest expenditure by local government is for public education, which is mandated by the state. The largest state expenditures are usually for health and hospitals, public education, and welfare, all of which are extremely difficult to trim because of legislation on the books, public support, and growing public demand. Further, many expenditures are tied into federal programs, and state cuts would cause a reduction in the federal contribution to a joint venture.[12] Agency programs, in other words, enjoy a good deal of insulation from the efforts of those who would change them through the budgetary process.

In forty-five states, the governor is given the budget-making authority, which means that he reviews agency spending requests and presents his budget recommendations to the legislature. In two executive-budget states, Florida and West Virginia, he shares authority with a board on which he and other elected cabinet-level officials sit. In Mississippi and South Carolina, budgetary authority rests with a combined legislative-executive commission; in Arkansas, a legislative council is responsible for budget preparation, although an executive office provides a great deal of assistance. Although, with these exceptions, the authority to compile the basic budget document is in the hands of the governor, in another nine states he lacks complete formal authority over central budget office officials. This means that the budget staff may not be very responsive to his desires, even though he is free to overrule their recommendations.

The median number of professional staff analysts in state budget offices is ten, ranging from one or two in five small states to over a hundred in both California and New York. In addition to budget analysis, they carry on other closely related activities. For example, in over thirty states they are responsible for preparing revenue estimates and for management analysis, which encompasses the study of and recommendation on administrative systems and procedures and organizational structure. Other state budget agencies perform functions such as accounting, preauditing,[13] and data processing.

When the executive presents the budget to the legislature, it is generally reviewed by an appropriations committee rather than a specific subject-area committee such as education or health. The appropriations committee is aided by a small professional staff, consisting of three or fewer persons in most states. Some legislatures are constitutionally constrained in their budgetary actions. In eight states, the legislature may not appropriate more than the state receives in revenues. In eight states, also, a general appropriation bill must be passed before any other appropriation bill. In three states the legislature may not increase spending for given items above the governor's recommendation, unless it enacts separate bills. The governor has the authority to use an item veto in appropriations bills in three-quarters of the states.[14]

The role perceptions of the following key actors in the state budgetary policy process can be summarized as follows:[15]

1. *Line agency administrators.* Such officials ordinarily desire expansion of their budgets, though the extent to which they may ask for more funds varies a great deal. One study found that while almost one-half of state executives desired budgetary increases of more than 10 percent for their agency, one-quarter wanted increases of less than 10 percent, and another quarter wanted no increase at all.[16] The types of state executives

discussed in Chapter 1 have different attitudes toward budgetary growth: program executives are most likely to desire substantial expansion of budgets and programs, while policy executives, political executives, and popular executives, in declining order, are less likely to favor such a course.[17] It is usually necessary for the administrator to seek larger budgets not only because of population growth and inflation but also because of the need to satisfy several "audiences"—the agency's employees, the agency's clientele groups, and the officials who review the budget requests. Requests for more funds underline the significance and protect the status of agency employees, assure clientele groups that new and higher standards are being pursued, and ease the burdens felt by reviewing officials in dealing with programs about which they may have little or no knowledge. If an agency does not ask for more money or if it returns funds, it may well have its budget cut on the grounds that it does not need the money.[18] Thus, for all these reasons it is necessary to "pad" the budget somewhat.

2. *Central budget office review officers.* These officers are oriented toward reducing agencies' requests, because of the audiences to which they must pay attention. They consider it more important to act as watchdogs of the treasury than as assistants to the agencies in discharging their responsibilities more economically and effectively; that is, they consider their control function to be more important than their management function.[19] Legislators and the governor expect the review officers to make cuts, and if they do not do so they would be challenging the justification of the existence of overhead agencies. Further, they know they can reduce incremental requests of the agencies without affecting essential operations, and thus adequate services are not threatened.

3. *Governors.* One writer argues that the governor has little effect on the budgetary policy-making process for two reasons: the inexperience in state financial matters of most governors upon assumption of office, and the complexity of the state's bookkeeping system. Illinois has 40 special funds besides the general fund, and Oregon has 168. Three-fifths of the states finance upwards of half their total expenditures from such funds, which are restricted to certain programs, such as highway construction, and cannot be diverted.

The governor's position in the budgetary policy-making process has been compared to that of a blind man on top of a mountain who is trying to affect its height and mass by moving pebbles near the summit. Although this simile is exaggerated, because a governor determined either to raise or to lower expenditures may well have some impact, the constraints on him are more salient than any freedom of action or power he may have. A conservative like California's Governor Reagan is able to slow the growth rate of the state budget, but he cannot reduce its absolute size. A liberal governor like New York's Rockefeller is able to increase substantially expenditures in selected areas like higher education, but only up to a point, and finds many other areas of the budget outside his control.

4. *Legislators.* As mentioned above, most legislators lack expertise to deal with the budget. Thus, their options consist of either approving figures recommended by the governor or indiscriminately cutting his recommendations. Rarely do legislators significantly increase the total budget. The legislature, then, is not a particularly potent actor in the budgetary process.

An examination of the budgetary process in nineteen states sheds further light on the relative weight of actors in the budgetary process. The size of the agency's request influences both the governor's recommendation and the legislature's appropriation; agencies asking for substantial increases receive severe short-term treatment, whereas agencies requesting rather modest increases are much more likely to receive what they want.[20] Agencies that manage to expand their budget significantly apparently need to make requests for substantial increases over a period of time. The study indicates that the governor's recommendation is more important for the legislature than is the size of the agency request to the governor in determining the final amount appropriated. However, one must conclude that if any one actor is more powerful in this process than the others, it would seem to be the agencies (and their attendant clientele groups), since those agencies seeking modest increases are generally treated well by the governor and the legislature, while those asking for large increases suffer the greatest reductions in the short run, but may well gain in the long run.[21]

POLICY DEVELOPMENT: CITY BUDGETING

Although available evidence indicates that the politics of the budgetary process at the urban level is very similar to that at the state level (agencies as the initiators and agenda-setters, with the chief executive more important than the legislature in determining the final appropriation), some additional insights can be gained through an examination of studies of city budgeting.

Research on the budgetary process in Cleveland, Detroit, and Pittsburgh, all cities of over 500,000 population, produced a simulation model of a budgetary system with a number of characteristics. In the three cities, the problem in budget making that confronts the chief executive is to produce a budget that is in balance, maintains existing service levels, provides, if possible, for employee wage raises, and avoids tax increases.[22] When the chief executive is convinced that it is necessary to cut costs, there are well-defined priorities. Maintenance and equipment are the first to go; operating expenses, supplies, and materials are next. Only after all the foregoing have been trimmed are salaries and wages reduced.[23] The decision rules used by actors in these cities are internalized and, to a large extent, insulated from external pressures. The decision system is responsive only to special revenue opportunities, to long-run, cumulative political pressures, or to a short-run, catastrophic event.[24]   In other words, the system is not much subject to public pressure, but rather, is closed and autonomous. A study of four smaller New England cities, however, found that external interest groups play a significant role in the political process and that the mayor plays a lesser role here than he does in the larger cities.[25]   The Cleveland-Detroit-Pittsburgh data indicate that the city council rubber-stamped decisions made by the executive. A study of council budget cutting in the San Francisco area discovered that councilmen share basic norms regarding which programs should be cut. Most councilmen mention as "untouchables" fire and police protection, sewerage and water, and other publicly owned utilities; they are more willing to cut back on amenities (libraries, education, or planning), because they consider these programs to be less valuable.[26]

There are some interesting variations in budget making in large manager cities, depending upon whether the mayoralty is simply rotated among members of the city council or is elective. Research into manager governments of cities of over 100,000 population indicates that in those with elected mayors, the manager typically must share much more power in the budgetary process with the mayor than is the case when the mayor is not independently elected. Cities with elected mayor-managers are characterized by more bargaining and agreement on policy outside and prior to the formal budgetary process, more examination of program areas in detail, and discussion of a larger number of policy areas by the council. Partisan elections, awareness of party affiliations, and party endorsement of council candidates are all related to less influence by the manager, while nonpartisan elections, true nonpartisanship, and the absence of party endorsement are related to greater managerial influence.[27]

Although some studies cited above stress the power of the chief executive in budget making, it seems impossible to conclude that any actor is more important than the line agencies in the budgetary process. Even large cities ordinarily have small budget staffs; the Pittsburgh mayor's office, for example, has a budget staff of four for a budget of more than $75 million, with thousands of items.[28]   The study of New England cities found the situation to be even more marked, since "the absence of skilled and highly trained professionals was the rule, not the exception."[29]   Oakland, California, has a high turnover in its small budget agency staff.[30]   Thus, while the chief executive's budget recommendations may be accepted by the city council, the chief executive himself is unable to make any kind of meaningful review of the budget requests of the line agencies. In cities with an adequate budgetary staff to assist the chief executive, such as New York, the informal political dynamics of alliances among agency heads, interest groups, and legislative allies may prevent him from exercising much control over the budget. For example, in a period of financial crisis, New York's Mayor John Lindsay was unable in repeated attempts to delete the appropriation for the sanitation department's musical band.[31]

While the overall characteristics of the city budget process resemble those found at the state level, the research discussed above deals with an almost bewildering variety of behavior shown by different actors. Not until much more data are available will it be possible to generalize, for example, about which kinds of interest groups, in which kinds of cities, in which issue areas, under which kinds of conditions, wield crucial budget-making power.

POLICY IMPLEMENTATION: STATE AND CITY GOVERNMENTS

Budgetary fund implementation takes place in the allotment of appropriated funds to the line agencies. It is dominated by the agencies, central budget office, and the chief executive in most states, because legislatures rarely have sufficient staff or the audit authority that would allow them to play a significant part. In those states where the legislature does have adequate audit authority, the auditors may be two or three years behind in their work due to lack of supporting personnel. Moreover, most government do not yet employ performance auditing, which, like PPBS, evaluates the efficiency of agencies in policy implementation. Legislatures that run a well-staffed performance audit can play a key role in the policy implementation process.

Although the chief executive and his overhead agencies usually have authority to determine how much of the legislative appropriation actually goes to the agency, they cannot withhold funds without cause; they must cite revenue constraints or inability of the agency to use the funds. But a chief executive who wishes to cut budgets can follow certain tactics to circumvent legal restrictions. Because he and the central budget office usually have authority to disburse allotments at any rate they desire, he may distribute quarterly allotments at a rate under 25 percent, and then give all remaining funds to the agency in the last quarter. Usually, the agency, having pared down its operations for most of the year, will be unable to spend all of its final-quarter allotment, so the chief executive will have in effect made a budget cut.

The agencies themselves, on the other hand, usually have a great deal of discretion in spending, since the categories under which funds are appropriated (personnel, equipment, supplies) are broad enough to enable an agency to move funds around within categories and spend them for purposes very different from those intended. No central agency is large enough to monitor all of an agency's expenditures. Thus, as far as budget implementation is concerned, the lion's share of power seems to lie in the hands of the implementers.

Factors Associated with Expenditure Patterns

It is impossible to overemphasize the great range in the policies of city and state governments. Some of the differences are obvious; poor states like Mississippi do not spend as much on governmental services as do rich states like New York. However, there are a number of relevant questions unexplained by such variables. For example, the number of employees of state and local governments per 10,000 population varies enormously among some states that are very similar socioeconomically. At the same time, however, "wealthy" Pennsylvania and "poor" South Carolina have almost the same ratio of combined state and local employees to population.[32]

In recent years a large body of social science literature concerning the factors associated with patterns of government expenditures has been written. Yet, as is so often the case with the social sciences, there is still no clear pattern in the literature that enables the reader to conclude confidently that certain types of variables are more important than others in determining expenditure patterns for state and urban governments. The initial wave of research indicated that the key variables associated with higher levels of government spending were social and economic factors correlated with increased wealth—for example, income, occupation, economic base of the community, urbanism, and industrialism. The message was that political variables such as structure and form of government, political party relationships, and electoral systems had no impact on expenditure levels.[33] Later work, however, casts doubt on these assertions. One study, for example, reports that the redistribution of income through government policies indicates that "political variables employed in the model are considerably more important than the socio-economic variables in explaining inter-state variations in redistributive patterns."[34] Another study also concludes that "the role of inter-party competition in affecting state policy should not, then, be unduly downgraded."[35]

Investigations of the relationship between governmental form and budget output have been indefinite. Research has found no relationship at the state level.[36] Much more attention has been paid to the association between city reform and nonreform types of government and spending, but the conclusions have been unclear. Some research has found correlations between the form of government and the type of government policies and expenditure levels,[37] while other research has not.[38]

Conclusion

The budgetary process involves a struggle for power among the key actors in bureaucratic politics. Although bureaucrats in effect set the agenda, other actors have substantial power to affect the ultimate size and shape of the budget. Unfortunately, it is difficult at present to generalize about which actors tend to prevail under which conditions.

CHAPTER NINE

Bureaucracy and the Public

The performance of government agencies in the United States is under more vehement attack now than has ever previously been the case. As President Nixon remarked in his 1971 State of the Union Message, "Most Americans today are simply fed up with government at all levels." A prominent scholar has argued that we have a "bureaucracy problem."[1] What is its nature and what can be done about it?

Actually there are several bureaucracy problems: *accountability*, or control, assuring that bureaucrats serve the goals set for them by law-makers; *equity*, or equal treatment for everyone, based on rules known in advance; *efficiency*, or the attainment of goals at minimum cost; *responsiveness*, or swift and humane action in granting exceptions, where appropriate, to general rules; and *fiscal integrity*, or the proper spending of appropriations. Different groups have their own degrees of concern for each problem. Chief executives are most interested in accountability; lawyers and courts in equity; business and taxpayer groups in efficiency; individuals, party leaders, and legislators in responsiveness; and legislative and chief executive overhead agencies in fiscal integrity.

Exacerbating the bureaucracy problems is the frequent lack of clearly stated bureau program goals, which usually results from the nature of a bureau's political setting. If the bureau is primarily concerned with organization maintenance or must serve several clientele groups, it may be unable, even if pressed, to articulate goals. Attempts to solve the five bureaucracy problems listed above will accomplish little if bureau goals are not explicitly stated and logically consistent.

The bureaucracy problems of most concern to the public today can be divided into two broad areas: citizen control of the bureaucracy and bureau problem-solving ability. The first area includes the problems of accountability, equity, and responsiveness. The second includes not only the problem of clear statement of goals but also the attempt to develop and implement policy to reach these goals. While efficiency and fiscal integrity are the concern of a number of people, they are not as urgent to the public as the problems in these two areas.

HOW TO INCREASE CITIZEN CONTROL OF THE BUREAUCRACY

A number of critics view modern bureaucracies as autonomous power centers, indifferent to or contemptuous of public reaction to their policies.

George Wallace focused on resentment of this perceived situation in his 1968 and 1972 campaigns, when he talked about "bearded, beatnik bureaucrats" and their allies, "pointy-headed intellectuals," who allegedly devised school busing and integration policies with no thought for those affected. A leading critique of contemporary society charges that the United States Has become an administrative state, in which decision making has been taken from citizens and given to professional bureaucrats.[2]

Whether or not these sweeping indictments are accurate, a good deal of evidence does exist that the poor and the ethnic and racial minorities have little influence over the bureaucracies they confront. First of all, they are handicapped by ignorance of the system and tend to be intimidated by the rules.[3] Second, even when they do become knowledgeable enough to try to change things, they may find that the tactics of middle-class groups do not work for them. Two examples illustrate the point.

In a widespread 1964 "strike" in New York City, tenants refused to pay rent because buildings allegedly had not been maintained at a standard that assured health and safety. Many demonstrations, characterized by picketing and speeches, took place. The agencies with jurisdiction over housing took a number of measures but never carried out policies that they had full legal authority to implement and that would have alleviated matters much more directly: the city was empowered to make repairs on privately owned buildings and to receive payment for the repairs from landlords.[4]

A study of rent strikes in Newark, New Jersey, showed that the tenant leaders were quickly evicted, while laws mandating proper maintenance by landlords were not enforced. As the author of the study concludes, "The ghetto residents learned what many always had suspected: some laws, such as those dealing with the collection or rents, the eviction of tenants, and the protection of property were swiftly enforceable, while other laws, such as those dealing with flagrant violations of building and safety codes and protection of people, were unaccountably unenforceable."[5] Residents in a middle-class neighborhood were able to get a traffic light installed 28 days after submitting a petition with approximately 50 signatures, while black ghetto residents were unable to get a light with a petition of 350 signatures, a block rally, letters and calls to city hall, interrupting traffic, and picketing at the intersection.

The cause of this differential response seems to lie in a clash of social-class cultures. Bureaucrats, who are predominantly middle class, often lack sympathy and understanding for their lower-class clients, whom they view as morally deficient.[6] Furthermore, a bureau may be handicapped by a large number of such clients, because it may then be harder to attain its goals. For example, government job-training programs often exclude those most in need of help, such as former convicts, because experience suggests that such persons have a high rate of failure—which reflects on the bureau.

As minority groups and the poor have grown politically conscious and politically active, they have pressed for more influence vis-à-vis the bureaucracy, in part, by demanding new or changed structures, such as increased membership on boards, a traditional device used throughout American history to gain access to the political process; the establishment of ombudsmen or review commissions to investigate complaints about government agencies; and decentralization, or the devolution to neighborhood councils of control of government operations in their areas.[7]

What prospects are there that the reforms will end citizen disillusionment with government? These proposals, like any others, have both benefits and costs; and only the individual citizen can decide, in terms of his own preferences, whether they are "good" or "bad."

Minority representation is the demand most often met, which is to be expected, for it involves the least radical change. Although chief executives today are much more willing to appoint to boards persons from ethnic groups, they are unlikely to select either radical or poor persons from those groups. Moreover, minority-group representatives will not become the majority on a board until those they represent become the majority in the community. There is little that a few members of a board can do other than attract media coverage through outspoken criticism of the status quo.

Specialized citizen review boards, such as police review boards, do exist in some communities and, no doubt, can have real impact on bureaucratic behavior. Nevertheless, they are unlikely to become common—or to have substantial minority membership—until the community as a whole has significant numbers of minority citizens. The office of ombudsman,[8] or an official empowered to investigate complaints of any aspect of government within a jurisdiction, has been established in at least five states, as well as in several cities. An ombudsman is limited by lack of staff and expertise, as well as the power to enforce his decisions. While the ombudsman can only make recommendations, most of the state ombudsmen feel that agencies are generally responsive to their recommendations.[9] Although the ombudsman may make the system more just, there is the possibility that his input may constitute exceptions to rules, thus causing less consistency and more fragmentation in the system. And certainly the ombudsman is unlikely to make great changes or major decisions in the system without the strong support of other, more powerful actors.

Decentralization is the most radical demand for organizational change. Decentralization characterized the antipoverty program, which created new community and neighborhood agencies that allowed the poor to play a key role. The area in which there has been the greatest call for decentralization is city public education, the most dramatic example being New York.[10] Attempts to decentralize one area in 1968 failed after a teachers' strike, but the demand for decentralization is mounting again there and in other central cities. Advocates of decentralization argue that it would increase support of the political system by giving have-not groups access to decision making, enhance the individual's sense of well-being through his heightened participation in the system, lead to greater efficiency for overly large bureaucracies, increase accountability and control, and upgrade bureaucratic performance by making bureaucrats more aware of the needs of their clients.

The appeals of decentralization are strong ones to the disgruntled citizen. He is offered a chance to exert a measure of control over agency operations that directly affect his life. But there are also costs to decentralization, including the following:

1. *Locale.* Decentralization may be a boon to a minority group in New York City, but similar groups in Alabama or Mississippi may suffer even more discrimination under such reorganization.

2. *Participation.* Evidence to date indicates that the smaller the governmental unit, the less participation, whether measured by voting or some other index such as activity in community decision making. New York City local school board elections, the national experience with anti-poverty board elections, and the literature on community politics all support this generalization.[11] Perhaps this pattern would change if all key governmental functions were decentralized.

3. *Higher financial costs.* Decentralization necessitates the creation of local representative bodies and bureaus, which results in increased costs. This parallel, overlapping structure is unlikely to displace any bureaucrats at higher levels and lead to economies there.[12]

4. *Delay in decision making.* Greater participation by neighborhood groups slows down the decision-making process, even if relatively small numbers of people are involved.

5. *Increased fragmentation.* Decentralized structures increase fragmentation and thus inevitably reduce coordination and consistency in the system.

6. *Increased polarization.* Decentralized structures may well tend to exacerbate conflict in socially and ethnically heterogeneous neighborhoods and thus lead to an exodus of middle-class groups. Such a pattern occurred again and again in local antipoverty organizations when one group took over the program and tried to exclude others.[13]

Some of the original proponents of decentralization have become disenchanted. Kenneth Clark, a black psychologist and educator, declared in May, 1972, that New York City's school decentralization was failing because local boards were more interested in gaining power than in improving education.[14] Like any other organizational reform, then, decentralization has both costs and benefits, and it is not a panacea for whatever problems ail a community.

An alternative approach to increased citizen control is coordination by the chief executive. Proponents of "executive leadership" argue that increased coordination is the only way to make government more responsive to the people, and that extensive reorganization, with all power to the chief executive, is the means to such an end.

This change also has costs as well as benefits. There will inevitably be overlap and lack of coordination in a pluralistic society of great heterogeneity in which many types of groups are politically active. Disparate groups will work to establish agencies that will operate in their behalf. In government reorganization designed to coordinate services, it is often those agencies serving the interests of the disadvantaged and the poor that are eliminated or subjected to tremendous attrition. This happens because they lack political support sufficient to sustain them in the face of reorganization, while the more powerful lobbies and alliances of political actors are able to maintain agencies that serve the interests of more privileged groups.[15] Thus, one sees slashes in state welfare benefits in the 1970s, while highway agencies continue to receive much the same kind of budgets as in the past. This differential treatment is not accidental; it is directly attributable to the political strength of the interest group clientele and allies of the agencies involved.

BUREAUCRATIC GOALS AND GOAL ATTAINMENT

Several writers have recently argued that the principal bureaucracy problem is not how to reduce bureaucratic power, but how to define clearly the key problems and to take the steps necessary to meet them.[16] Whether we retain our present political system or adopt a fascist, communist, or anarchist system, we will still have to deal with problems like environmental pollution, inner-city decay, drug addiction, and a lagging economy. And it remains an alarming fact that we do not have solutions to many of the problems confronting us.[17] Concerning the question of welfare, almost all Americans are agreed that the present system is a failure, but there is no consensus on what the goal of welfare policy should be. Should it be a decent standard of living for all, a job for all, or a reduction in the welfare rolls as much as possible? It is unfair to blame this disparity of views on bureaucrats alone, since all actors in this system are divided. Even if something like goal consensus is reached, bureaucrats must devise a means of reaching the goal. We do not know, for example, whether guaranteed annual income schemes, "workfare," or minor reforms in the existing structure would be the best way to attain any of the three goals stated above. Although a number of local experiments have been testing different methods, the solution to this problem is not yet in sight. Nor is it in sight in education, health, corrections, transportation, or any other policy area. The need to run pilot programs to get some idea of the efficacy of proposed solutions is pressing, but such pilot programs are rarely carried out. Instead, vast programs are launched with little idea of what they will yield. The 1960s proved that large amounts of money do not cure social ills like ghetto unemployment. Indeed, it is not even apparent that technological problems, such as pollution, can be corrected without basic changes in current life style and living standards.

TACTICS TO INFLUENCE THE BUREAUCRACY

What can the individual do to try to solve the particular bureaucracy problem that means the most to him? First, he can support candidates who share his concern with this bureaucracy problem, and he can urge chief executives and legislators to reorganize the bureaucracy and pressure it to be more responsive. While this approach may yield some dividends, it is necessary to concentrate on the bureaus themselves, since they are often autonomous power centers. As already noted, legislators and chief executives have many interests besides specific program goals.

Second, he can support groups trying to bring about changes in bureau cultures and procedures. One approach used to influence the bureaucracy is the confrontation strategy of neighborhood organizers who seek to motivate have-not groups to participate in solving problems that confront them. Organizers try to get people together to do something about a relatively small grievance, such as the refusal by a welfare bureaucrat to buy furniture for a recipient when the recipient is entitled by law to this benefit. Bringing protesters into the welfare office or picketing it may well bring some action. This kind of approach has been used successfully by the National Welfare Rights Organization.[18]

Lawyers are key staff members or allies of organizing groups, because they may be able to win a court order to compel the bureaucrat if all other tactics fail. The legal approach is exemplified by the federal legal services program, which provides legal assistance to the poor, enabling them to take bureaucrats to court. Likewise, "advocate planners" offer their technical expertise to the disadvantaged, rather than to bureaus.[19] Similar tactics are employed by consumer groups, such as those led by Ralph Nader, which file suits on behalf of the public in cases concerning pollution or defective goods, where they argue that the public good is being irreparably damaged.

Attempts to form a coalition of middle-class liberals to act as a countervailing force to the bureaucracy resulted in Common Cause, a group that attempts, through Washington and state capital lobbyists as well as grassroots organizing, to channel citizen discontent into a force for constructive change. Although it is difficult to point to any substantial victories by

Common Cause, there is no reason such a group—right-wing, left-wing, or centrist—could not exert considerable influence if it had enough membership support.

A number of younger bureaucrats have taken the position that they should work primarily to help have-not groups. They do not even pretend to be neutral administrators, but see themselves as explicit proponents of policy. These public administrators argue that "social equity," or equal treatment for all with whom they deal, must be the foremost goal of the bureaucrat.[20]   To this breed of bureaucrat, the optional strategy is to "infiltrate" a bureau and move it from within toward the new culture of social equity.

Whatever approach one selects to solve his bureaucracy problem, he must labor hard to make any progress. No major changes can occur overnight. Bureaucrats and their allies are full-time actors, with a great stake in the bureau's culture. But the bureaucracy is no more impervious than it is monolithic. Those who want to influence bureaucratic behavior can do so if they devote themselves to the task in sufficient numbers.

Conclusion

Americans of all political persuasions seem increasingly discontented with government bureaucracy today. At the same time, no consensus exists regarding the direction in which change should occur. Since bureaucracy cannot be abolished, an increasing number of political actors are trying to influence bureaucratic behavior through different means.

Notes

INTRODUCTION

1. Morris Janowitz, Deil S. Wright, and William Delaney, *Public Administration and the Public: Perspectives Toward Government in a Metropolitan Community* (Ann Arbor: Bureau of Government, University of Michigan, 1958), p. 2.

2. Herbert Jacob and Michael Lipsky, "Outputs, Structure, and Power: An Assessment of Changes in the Study of State and Local Politics," *Journal of Politics* 30 (May 1968): 523.

3. Half the total number of urban and state employees are in education. Since some of the urban and state employees work part-time, the full-time equivalent equals 8.5 million workers.

1. ADMINISTRATIVE AGENCIES AND BUREAUCRATS

1. *See* David T. Stanley and Associates, *Professional Personnel for the City of New York* (Washington, D.C.: Brookings Institution, 1963).

2. David Rogers, *110 Livingston Street* (New York: Random House, 1968), pp. 285-90.

3. Frederick C. Mosher, *Democracy and the Public Service* (New York: Oxford University Press, 1968), pp. 106-7.

4. Cf. Anthony Downs, *Inside Bureaucracy* (Boston: Little, Brown, 1967), pp. 237-46.

5. Ibid., pp. 228-31.

6. Ibid., pp. 233-36.

7. Ibid., p. 226.

8. James Q. Wilson, *Varieties of Police Behavior* (Cambridge: Harvard University Press, 1968).

9. Cf. Downs, *Inside Bureaucracy*, pp. 88-111.

10. Michael Lipsky, "Street-Level Bureaucracy and the Analysis of Urban Reform," in Virginia B. Ermer and John H. Strange, eds., *Blacks and Bureaucracy* (New York: Crowell, 1972), pp. 171-84.

11. Two good recent works on the topic are Sam Zagoria, ed., *Public Workers and Public Unions* (Englewood Cliffs, N.J.: Prentice-Hall, 1972); and David T. Stanley, *Managing Local Government Under Union Pressure* (Washington, D.C.: Brookings Institution, 1972).

12. Wallace S. Sayre and Herbert Kaufman, *Governing New York City* (New York: Russell Sage, 1960), pp. 267-68.

13. *See* Frances Fox Piven, "Militant Civil Servants in New York City," *Trans-Action* 8 (November 1969): 24-28, 55.

14. Cf. Downs, *Inside Bureaucracy*, p. 215.

15. *See* Edward C. Banfield and James Q. Wilson, *City Politics* (Cambridge: Harvard University Press, 1963), pp. 138-42.

16. E. Lester Levine, J. Terry Edwards, and David H. Pingree, "The Response of Florida Administrators to Change" (Paper delivered at the Annual Conference of the American Society for Public Administration, Philadelphia, 8 April 1970), p. 19.

17. Deirdre Carmody, "Murphy Denounces Civil Service," *New York Times*, 15 January 1972, p. 1.

18. Committee for Economic Development, *Modernizing State Government* (New York: Committee for Economic Development, 1967), pp. 88-89.

19. *See* Arthur E. Buck, *The Reorganization of State Governments in the United States* (New York: Columbia University Press, 1938), pp. 14-28. The reader will note the contradictions in the reform movement, which has espoused both agency autonomy and coordinated government during its history.

20. *See State Executive Reorganization* (Chicago: Council of State Governments, 1969); and Karl A. Bosworth, "The Politics of Management Improvement in the States," *American Political Science Review* 47 (1953): 84-99. See Charles R. Adrian and Charles Press, *Governing Urban America* (New York: McGraw-Hill, 1968), pp. 305-6, for further consideration of the difficulties in achieving reorganization.

21. George A. Bell, "States Make Progress with Reorganization Plans," *National Civic Review*, March 1972, pp. 115-19, 127. *See also* two 1970 publications of the Council of State Governments (Lexington, Ky.): *Coordination of State Activities* and *Organization for Management Improvement Activities in the States*.

22. Thomas Dye, "Executive Power and Public Policy in the States," *Western Political Quarterly* 22 (December 1969): 932.

23. Deil S. Wright, "Executive Manpower for Indeterminate Government: Staffing the States" (Paper presented at the Annual Conference of the American Society for Public Administration, New York, 24 March 1972), pp. 8-10.

24. Deil S. Wright and Richard L. McAnaw, "American State Executives: Their Backgrounds and Careers," *State Government* 38 (summer 1965): 153.

25. Fred W. Grupp and Allan R. Richards, "Partisan Political Activity Among American State Executives" (Paper presented at the Annual Meeting of the American Political Science Association, Chicago, 7-11 September 1971). See the authors' forthcoming volume, *The American State Executive*.

26. In New York City, for example, the key decision-making body is the Board of Estimate, made up of the mayor and seven other city officials, which overshadows the council.

27. Robert J. Mowitz and Deil S. Wright, *Profile of a Metropolis* (Detroit: Wayne State University Press, 1962), pp. 579-628.

28. York Willbern, "Personnel and Money," in James W. Fesler, ed., *The 50 States and Their Local Governments* (New York: Knopf, 1967), p. 375.

29. *The Municipal Yearbook*, published annually by the International City Management Association, is the most valuable compendium of information on American urban government administration. The equivalent publication for the states is *The Book of the States*, published every other year by the Council of State Governments.

30. *See* Peter Allen, "Career Patterns of Top Executives in New York City Government," *Public Personnel Review* 33 (April 1972): pp. 114-17.

31. Edward C. Banfield, *Political Influence* (Glencoe, Ill.: Free Press, 1961), p. 266.

32. Russell D. Murphy, *Political Entrepreneurs and Urban Poverty* (Lexington, Mass.: Heath, 1971), p. 11.

33. M. Kent Jennings, "Public Administrators and Community Decision-Making," *Administrative Science Quarterly* 8 (June 1963): 18-43.

34. Linton Freeman et al., "Locating Leaders in Local Communities," *American Sociological Review* 28 (October 1963): 791-98; Roscoe C. Martin et al., *Decisions in Syracuse* (Garden City, N.Y.: Doubleday, Anchor Books, 1965), p. 324; and Conrad Joyner, "Tucson," in Leonard E. Goodall, ed., *Urban Politics in the Southwest* (Tempe, Ariz.: Institute of Public Administration, Arizona State University, 1967), pp. 165-95.

35. Mowitz and Wright, *Profile of a Metropolis*, p. 298.

36. Wilma Rule Krauss, "Some Aspects of the Influence Process of Public Bureaucrats," *Western Political Quarterly* 25 (June 1972): 323-39.

37. *See* Marilyn Gittell, "Education: The Decentralization-Community Control Controversy," in Jewel Bellush and Stephen M. David, eds., *Race and Politics in New York City* (New York: Praeger, 1971), pp. 134-63.

38. Deil S. Wright, "Governmental Forms and Planning Functions: The Relation of Organizational Structures to Planning Practice," in Thad L. Beyle and George T. Lathrop, eds., *Planning and Politics: Uneasy Partnership* (New York: Odyssey, 1970), pp. 68-105.

39. Think tanks are corporations engaged in contract consulting work, especially for government. *See* Harold Seidman, *Politics, Position and Power* (New York: Oxford University Press, 1970), pp. 256-68.

40. *See* Murphy, *Political Entrepreneurs and Urban Poverty*, p. 102.

41. Rufus P. Browning, "Innovative and Non-Innovative Decision Processes in Government Budgeting," in Robert T. Golembiewski, ed., *Public Budgeting and Finance* (Itasca, Ill.: Peacock, 1968), pp. 128-45. See also Martin et al., *Decisions in Syracuse;* and Downs, *Inside Bureaucracy*, pp. 88-111.

42. Virginia B. Ermer, "Housing Inspection in Baltimore," in Ermer and Strange, *Blacks and Bureaucracy*, pp. 83-93.

43. Edward N. Costikyan, *Behind Closed Doors* (New York: Harcourt, Brace, 1966), p. 293.

2. CHIEF EXECUTIVES

1. Leslie Lipson, *The American Governor: From Figurehead to Leader* (Chicago: University of Chicago Press, 1939). *See also* William H. Young, "The Development of the Governorship," *State Government* 31 (summer 1958): 178-83.

2. *See* Herbert Kaufman, "Emerging Conflicts in the Doctrines of Public Administration," *American Political Science Review* 50 (December 1956): 1057-73.

3. Gubernatorial vetoes are rarely overridden. *See* Frank W. Prescott, "The Executive Veto in American States," *Western Political Quarterly* 3 (1950): 99-112.

4. Malcolm E. Jewell, "The Governor as Legislative Leader," in Thad L. Beyle and J. Oliver Williams, eds., *The American Governor in Behavioral Perspective* (New York: Harper & Row, 1972), p. 128.

5. *See* John W. Lederle, "Governors and Higher Education," in Beyle and Williams, eds., *American Governor in Behavioral Perspective*, pp. 232-40, for an analysis of Reagan's changes in California's higher education policy.

6. Donald P. Sprengel, *Gubernatorial Staffs: Functional and Political Profiles* (Iowa City: Institute of Public Affairs, University of Iowa, 1969), p. 18.

7. Beyle and Williams, *American Governor in Behavioral Perspective*, pp. 2, 4.

8. Grants of formal authority can have great impact on *both* the development and implementation phases of policy making. Specific types of authority are listed in different sections because they are of greatest importance in the phase of policy making under which they are listed. As examples indicate, one type of authority may have impact on *both* phases of policy making.

9. Ira Sharkansky, "State Administrators in the Political Process," in Herbert Jacob and Kenneth N. Vines, eds., *Politics in the American States*, 2d ed. (Boston: Little, Brown, 1971), p. 249.

10. Joseph A. Schlesinger, "The Politics of the Executive," in Jacob and Vines, eds., *Politics in the American States*, p. 227.

11. Marshall W. Meyer, *Bureaucratic Structure and Authority* (New York: Harper & Row, 1972), p. 20.

12. Thad L. Beyle, "The Governor's Formal Powers: A View from the Governor's Chair," *Public Administration Review* 28 (November-December 1968): 540-45.

13. Alan J. Wyner, "Gubernatorial Relations with Legislators and Administrators," *State Government* 41 (summer 1968): 199-203.

14. Deil S. Wright, "Executive Leadership in State Administration: Interplay of Gubernatorial, Legislative and Administrative Power," *Midwest Journal of Political Science* 11 (February 1967): 13.

15. Coleman B. Ransone, Jr., *The Office of Governor in the United States* (University: University of Alabama Press, 1956), p. 238.

16. Robert B. Highsaw, "The Southern Governor—Challenge to the Strong Executive Theme," *Public Administration Review* 19 (winter 1959): 7-12.

17. Beyle and Williams, eds., *American Governor in Behavioral Perspective*, p. 2.

18. These systems are discussed in more detail in Chapter 8.

19. *See* Robert L. Chartrand, "The Governor and the New Systems Technology," in Beyle and Williams, eds., *American Governor in Behavioral Perspective*, p. 208; and the following publications of the Council of State Governments (Lexington, Ky.): *Central Management in the States* (1970), *Organization for Management Improvement Activities in the States* (1970), and *Coordination of State Activities* (1970).

20. Ransone, *Office of Governor*, pp. 135-36.

21. *Time*, 11 September 1972, p. 12.

22. Sprengle, *Gubernatorial Staffs*, pp. 24-25.

23. *See* Samuel R. Solomon, "Governors: 1960-1970," *National Civic Review* 60 (March 1971): 128-29, for the previous occupational background of governors. The great bulk is lawyers. Certainly the relatively low salary (averaging $29,000 in 1970) does not attract top administrators.

24. *The Municipal Yearbook, 1967* (Chicago: ICMA, 1967), pp. 104-5.

25. Russell M. Ross and Kenneth F. Millsap, "The Relative Power Position of Mayors in Mayor-Council Cities" (Iowa City: Laboratory for Political Research, University of Iowa, 1971), p. 16.

26. Robert J. Mowitz and Deil S. Wright, *Profile of a Metropolis* (Detroit: Wayne State University Press, 1962), p. 25.

27. *See* Robert A. Dahl, *Who Governs?* (New Haven: Yale University Press, 1961); Russell D. Murphy, *Political Entrepreneurs and Urban Poverty* (Lexington, Mass.: Heath, 1971); and Raymond A. Wolfinger, *The Politics of Progress* (Englewood Cliffs, N.J.: Prentice-Hall, forthcoming).

28. Jeffrey L. Pressman, "Preconditions of Mayoral Leadership," *American Political Science Review* 66 (June 1972): 511-24.

29. Duane Lockard, *The Politics of State and Local Government* (New York: Macmillan, 1963), pp. 417-27. Cf. James V. Cunningham, *Urban Leadership in the Sixties* (Waltham, Mass.: Lemberg Center for the Study of Violence, Brandeis University, 1970), which rates four mayors—Lee; Daley; Locher, of Cleveland; and Barr, of Pittsburgh—on "leadership."

30. Cf. the discussion of "arbiter" government in Charles R. Adrian and Oliver P. Williams, *Four Cities* (Philadelphia: University of Pennsylvania Press, 1963).

31. Robert Paul Boynton and Deil S. Wright, "Mayor-Manager Relationships in Large Council-Manager Cities: A Reinterpretation," *Public Administration Review* 31 (January-February 1971): 29.

32. Deil S. Wright, "The Dynamics of Budgeting—Large Council-Manager Cities," unpublished paper, 1969, p. 22. This finding does not necessarily mean that independently elected mayors gain power at the expense of the manager; rather, they may gain it at the expense of other actors, such as the council, the bureaucracy, or interest groups. *See* David A. Booth, "Are Elected Mayors a Threat to Managers?" *Administrative Science Quarterly* 13 (March 1968): 572-89.

33. Pressman, "Preconditions of Mayoral Leadership." Cf. Frank P. Sherwood and Beatrice Markey, "The Mayor and the Fire Chief," in Edwin A. Bock, ed., *State*

and Local Government: A Case Book (University: University of Alabama Press, 1963), pp. 109-34.

34. Karl Bosworth, "The Manager Is a Politician," *Public Administration Review* 18 (summer 1958): 216-22.

35. David A. Booth, *Council-Manager Government in Small Cities* (Chicago: ICMA, 1968), p. 105.

36. Ronald O. Loveridge, *City Managers in Legislative Politics* (Indianapolis: Bobbs-Merrill, 1971), p. 114.

37. B. James Kweder, *The Roles of the Manager, Mayor and Councilmen in Policy Making: A Study of 21 North Carolina Cities* (Chapel Hill: Institute of Government, University of North Carolina, 1965), pp. 31, 37. *See also* Charles R. Adrian, "A Study of Three Communities," *Public Administration Review* 18 (summer 1958): 208-13.

38. Pressman, "Preconditions of Mayoral Leadership."

39. Deil S. Wright, "The City Manager as a Development Administrator," in Robert T. Daland, ed., *Comparative Urban Research* (Beverly Hills, Ca.: Sage, 1969), p. 236. On the other hand, there are certainly a number who do seem to aim toward this goal.

40. Loveridge, *City Managers in Legislative Politics*, pp. 117-19. Cf. Boynton and Wright, "Mayor-Manager Relationships in Large Council-Manager Cities," p. 34.

41. Wolfinger, *Politics of Progress*, chap. 7.

42. See note 27 and Edward C. Banfield, *Political Influence* (Glencoe, Ill.: Free Press, 1961).

43. Murphy, *Political Entrepreneurs and Urban Poverty*, p. 11.

44. Op. cit., notes 29 and 31.

45. Pressman, "Preconditions of Mayoral Leadership."

46. Gladys M. Kammerer, "Role Diversity of City Managers," *Administrative Science Quarterly* 8 (March 1964): 421-42.

3. LEGISLATURES AND COURTS

1. *See* Herbert Kaufman, "Emerging Conflicts in Public Administration," *American Political Science Review* 50 (December 1956): 1057-73.

2. *See* Malcolm E. Jewell, "The Governor as Legislative Leader," in Thad L. Beyle and J. Oliver Williams, eds., *The American Governor in Behavioral Perspective* (New York: Harper & Row, 1972), p. 127; and Wallace S. Sayre and Herbert Kaufman, *Governing New York City* (New York: Russell Sage, 1960), p. 660.

3. In this role, legislators usually act as or with party organization leaders, as is noted in Chapter 4.

4. John Burns, *The Sometime Governments: A Critical Study of the 50 American Legislatures* (New York: Bantam, 1971).

5. Ibid., p. 5 and passim.

6. Although most of the state legislatures have had research staffs for some time, they have not played a key role in the policy process. For a description of them, *see* Malcom E. Jewell and Samuel C. Patterson, *The Legislative Process in the United States* (New York: Random House, 1966), pp. 251-52.

7. G. Theodore Mitau, *State and Local Government: Politics and Processes* (New York: Scribner, 1960), p. 29. The data were collected in 1950.

8. Burns, *Sometime Governments*, p. 4.

9. Elisabeth McK. Scott and Belle Zeller, "State Agencies and Lawmaking," *Public Administration Review* 2 (summer 1942): 205-20.

10. Arthur Bolton, "Expanding the Power of State Legislatures," in Donald G. Herzberg and Alan Rosenthal, eds., *Strengthening the States* (Garden City, N.Y.: Doubleday, 1971), pp. 61-72.

11. Burns, *Sometime Governments*, pp. 181-83, 193-96, 207-10, 268-72.

12. Ibid., p. 320.

13. Ibid., pp. 151-336.

14. *See Fiscal Services for State Legislatures* (Chicago: Council of State Governments, 1961).

15. *See The Book of the States, 1970-1971* (Lexington, Ky.: Council of State Governments, 1970), pp. 156-62.

16. *See* William J. Keefe, "The Functions and Powers of the State Legislatures," in Alexander Heard, ed., *State Legislatures in American Politics* (Englewood Cliffs, N.J.: Prentice-Hall, 1966), pp. 44-47.

17. "Executive Leadership in State Administration," *Midwest Journal of Political Science* 11 (February 1967): 4.

18. Rosaline Levenson, "Municipal Legislators: A Study of Attributes, Attitudes, and Job Satisfactions" (Ph.D. diss., University of Connecticut, 1971), pp. 220-21.

19. Sayre and Kaufman, *Governing New York City.*

20. Charles R. Adrian, "A Study of Three Communities," *Public Administration Review* 18 (summer 1958): 211-12.

21. B. James Kweder, *The Roles of the Manager, Mayor, and Councilmen in Policy Making: A Study of 21 North Carolina Cities* (Chapel Hill: Institute of Government, University of North Carolina, 1965), pp. 37-38, 96.

22. Ronald O. Loveridge, *City Managers in Legislative Politics* (Chicago: Rand McNally, 1971), p. 25, n. 20. Cf. David A. Booth, *Council-Manager Government in Small Cities* (Washington, D.C.: ICMA, 1968), p. 102.

23. Harry W. Reynolds, Jr., "The Career Public Service and Statute Lawmaking in Los Angeles," *Western Political Quarterly* 18 (September 1965): 638.

24. Edward C. Banfield, *Big City Politics* (New York: Random House, 1965), p. 82.

25. Ibid., p. 41.

26. Charles R. Adrian and Oliver P. Williams, *Four Cities* (Philadelphia: University of Pennsylvania Press, 1963), p. 208.

27. Deil S. Wright, "The Dynamics of Budgeting: Large Council-Manager Cities," unpublished paper, July 1969, p. 7.

28. Adrian, "A Study of Three Communities," p. 211.

29. None of the above should be construed to mean that councils are reluctant to remove managers. *See* Gladys Kammerer et al., *City Managers in Politics: An Analysis of Manager Tenure and Termination* (Gainesville: University of Florida Press, 1962).

30. Levenson, "Municipal Legislators," pp. 232, 237; and interview with Dr. Levenson, 4 February 1972.

31. Gladys M. Kammerer, "Role Diversity of City Managers," *Administrative Science Quarterly* 8 (March 1964): 421-42.

32. Banfield, *Big City Politics*, pp. 135-36.

33. *See* Theodore A. Driscoll, "Audit Called Key to Manager Government," *Hartford Courant*, 7 May 1972.

34. *See,* for example, Jack W. Peltason, *Federal Courts in the Political Process* (New York: Random House, 1955), pp. 13-17.

35. Martin Shapiro, *The Supreme Court and Administrative Agencies* (New York: Free Press, 1968).

36. Although other federal agencies are examined in Chapter 7, it seems appropriate to discuss the impact of courts at all three levels of government here.

37. *See* Richard M. Johnson, *The Dynamics of Compliance* (Evanston, Ill.: Northwestern University Press, 1967); and William K. Muir, Jr., *Prayer in the Public Schools* (Chicago: University of Chicago Press, 1967).

38. There are exceptions, but even then the court usually appoints an expert third party to devise a plan. Current examples include cases dealing with reapportionment and school busing and desegregation.

39. Kenneth M. Dolbeare, *Trial Courts in Urban Politics* (New York: Wiley, 1967), pp. 35, 38.

40. "Court Orders Prisons to Upgrade Hospitals," *Hartford Courant,* 5 October 1972.

4. POLITICAL PARTIES

1. That is, adoption of the reform package of council-manager government and nonpartisan elections did not in itself bring an end to corruption. *See* Edward C. Banfield and James Q. Wilson, *City Politics* (Cambridge: Harvard University Press, 1963), chaps. 9-13, conclusion.

2. The reformers allegedly slew the machine because it had increasingly less to offer city dwellers. *See* Fred I. Greenstein, *The American Party System and the American People,* 2d ed. (Englewood Cliffs, N.J.: Prentice-Hall, 1970), pp. 52-54. This doctrine of the conventional wisdom is provocatively disputed by Raymond Wolfinger, "Why Political Machines Have Not Withered Away and Other Revisionist Thoughts," *Journal of Politics* 34 (May 1972): 365-98; and Bruce M. Stave, *The New Deal and the Last Hurrah* (Pittsburgh: University of Pittsburgh Press, 1970).

3. Banfield and Wilson, *City Politics,* chap. 12.

4. Ibid.; and Eugene C. Lee, *The Politics of Nonpartisanship* (Berkeley: University of California Press, 1960).

5. Wallace S. Sayre and Herbert Kaufman, *Governing New York City* (New York: Russell Sage, 1960), p. 456.

6. Although executive branch patronage is of concern here, both the legislative and judicial branches are rich sources of patronage at the state and city levels. *See* Martin Tolchin and Susan Tolchin, *To the Victor: Political Patronage from the Clubhouse to the White House* (New York: Random House, 1971).

7. Calculated from data in *The Book of the States, 1970-1971* (Lexington, Ky.: Council of State Governments, 1970), pp. 170-73.

8. A number of civil service systems have been created by one political party to reduce the amount of patronage in agencies, such as those with elective heads, controlled by the opposition. *See* John H. Fenton, *Midwest Politics* (New York: Holt, Rinehart and Winston, 1966), p. 16.

Ira Sharkansky's analysis of the relationship between civil service coverage and government policy indicates that there is no strong correspondence between them. He found that states that give their employees the greatest coverage and compensation are unlikely to devote more resources to policy programs than are states that do less. *See* Sharkansky, "State Administrators in the Political Process," in Herbert Jacob and Kenneth N. Vines, eds., *Politics in the American States* (Boston: Little, Brown, 1971), pp. 238-71.

9. For additional information on Indiana party fund-raising practices, *see* Fenton, *Midwest Politics,* p. 164.

10. John Kifner, "Kickbacks Still Thrive in Indiana," *New York Times,* 11 July 1971, p. 21.

11. Martin Tolchin, "Political Patronage Rising at Fast Rate, Study Finds," *New York Times,* 17 June 1968, p. 1. *See also* Tolchin and Tolchin, *To the Victor.*

12. Tolchin and Tolchin, *To the Victor*, p. 103.

13. Martin Waldron, "Wallace Faces Mounting Criticism in Alabama over His Record, His Brother, and His Aides," *New York Times*, 5 May 1972, p. 26.

14. *The Municipal Yearbook*, 1967 (Chicago: ICMA, 1967), p. 165.

15. Tolchin and Tolchin, *To the Victor*, pp. 71-72.

16. Tolchin, "Political Patronage Rising at Fast Rate." Another new source of patronage is contracts given to consultants (cf. Chapter 6).

17. Wolfinger, "Why Political Machines Have Not Withered Away."

18. Robert K. Merton, *Social Theory and Social Structure*, rev. ed. (Glencoe, Ill.: Free Press, 1957), p. 72.

19. Wolfinger, "Why Political Machines Have Not Withered Away."

5. INTEREST GROUPS AND EMPLOYEE UNIONS

1. In his unpublished lectures.

2. I thank Robert S. Gilmour for this example.

3. Wallace S. Sayre and Herbert Kaufman, *Governing New York City* (New York: Russell Sage, 1960), pp. 279-85.

4. Ibid., pp. 264-69.

5. *See* James W. Fesler, *The Independence of State Regulatory Agencies* (Chicago: Public Administration Service, 1942).

6. Harold Seidman, *Politics, Position, and Power* (New York: Oxford University Press, 1970), pp. 138-46. Cf. Sayre and Kaufman, Governing New York City, p. 409.

7. *See* Gilbert Y. Steiner, *Social Insecurity: The Politics of Welfare* (Chicago: Rand McNally, 1966), chap. 7.

8. William W. Keifer, "White Says He Won't Step Down," *Hartford Courant*, 20 October 1971.

9. This section is based on Sayre's unpublished lectures.

10. Thomas H. Eliot, "Reorganizing the Massachusetts Department of Conservation," in Edwin A. Bock, ed., *State and Local Government: A Case Book* (University: University of Alabama Press, 1963), pp. 315-36.

11. David A. Booth, *Council-Manager Government in Small Cities* (Chicago: ICMA, 1968), p. 110.

12. J. Leiper Freeman, *The Political Process* (New York: Random House, 1966), p. 88

13. Jerry Wurf, "The Revolution in Government Employment," in Robert H. Connery and William V. Farr, eds., "Unionization of Municipal Employees," *Proceedings of the Academy of Political Science* 30, no. 2 (1970): 134-45.

14. Harold Rubin, "Labor Relations in State and Local Governments," in Connery and Farr, "Unionization of Municipal Employees," pp. 14-28.

15. *See* Raymond D. Horton, "Municipal Labor Relations in New York City," in Connery and Farr, Unionization of Municipal Employees"; and A. H. Raskin, "Politics Up-Ends the Bargaining Table," in Sam Zagoria, ed., *Public Workers and Public Unions* (Englewood Cliffs, N.J.: Prentice-Hall, 1972), pp. 122-46.

16. This section and the rest of the chapter are based principally on David T. Stanley, *Managing Local Government Under Union Pressure* (Washington, D.C.: Brookings Institution, 1972).

17. Ibid., p. 111.

18. Ibid., p. 145.

19. Frederick O'R. Hayes, "Collective Bargaining and the Budget Director," in Zagoria, *Public Workers and Public Unions*, p. 89.

20. Stanley, *Managing Local Government Under Union Pressure*, pp. 140-41.

21. Ibid., pp. 139-40.

6. COMMUNICATIONS MEDIA AND ADVISORY GROUPS

1. It is hoped that there will soon be a good monograph on television news reporting at any level of government, following the direction of Paul H. Weaver in his superb "Is Television News Biased?" *Public Interest* (winter, 1972), pp. 57-74.

2. *See* Delmar D. Dunn, *Public Officials and the Press* (Reading, Mass.: Addison-Wesley, 1969), a study of reporters covering Wisconsin state government. Two previous studies that make similar points about Washington reporters are Douglass Cater, *The Fourth Branch of Government* (Boston: Houghton Mifflin, 1959); and Bernard C. Cohen, *The Press and Foreign Policy* (Princeton: Princeton University Press, 1963). The latter, by Dunn's mentor, provides the framework Dunn drew on for his analysis.

3. *See* M. Kent Jennings and Harmon Zeigler, "The Salience of American State Politics," *American Political Science Review* 64 (June 1970): p. 525.

4. Dunn, *Public Officials and the Press*, p. 55.

5. Edward C. Banfield and James Q. Wilson, *City Politics* (Cambridge: Harvard University Press, 1963), p. 322.

6. Russell Murphy, *Political Entrepreneurs and Urban Poverty* (Lexington, Mass.: Heath, 1971), p. 72. *See also* Morris Janowitz et al., *Public Administration and the Public: Perspectives toward Government in a Metropolitan Community* (Ann Arbor: Bureau of Government, University of Michigan, 1958), p. 97.

7. William Rivers, *The Adversaries: Politics and the Press* (Boston: Beacon Press, 1970). *See also* Dunn, *Public Officials and the Press*, pp. 95-96.

8. Dunn, *Public Officials and the Press*, p. 12.

9. Ibid., pp. 13-14.

10. Cohen, *The Press and Foreign Policy*, p. 13.

11. Scott Greer, *Metropolitics: A Study of Political Culture* (New York: Wiley, 1963), p. 113.

12. Cf. Dunn, *Public Officials and the Press*, p. 57.

13. Ibid., p. 76.

14. Cf. Bruce Smith, "The Future of Not-for-Profit Corporations," *Public Interest* 8 (summer 1967): 127-42; Paul Dickson, *Think Tanks* (New York: Atheneum, 1971); and Frederick Hayes and John E. Rasmussen, eds., *Centers for Innovation for State and Local Government* (San Francisco: San Francisco Press, 1973).

15. *See* Dickson, *Think Tanks*, pp. 239-47.

16. "PSB Rules Against Underground Cables," *Rutland Daily Herald*, 28 July 1972.

17. *See* Bruce L. R. Smith, *The RAND Corporation* (Cambridge: Harvard University Press, 1966).

18. Cf. Robert J. Mowitz and Deil S. Wright, *Profile of a Metropolis* (Detroit: Wayne State University Press, 1962), p. 231.

19. *Policy on Use of Consultants in State Government* (Lexington, Ky.: Council of State Governments, 1968), p. 1.

20. Ibid., p. 16 (page is unnumbered).

21. Interview with Deil S. Wright, 12 September 1972.

22. See the following for a discussion of the knowledge explosion: Warren G. Bennis, "Post-Bureaucratic Leadership," *Trans-Action*, July-August 1969, pp. 44-51, 61; Allen Schick, "The Cybernetic State," *Trans-Action*, February 1970, pp. 14-26; and Alvin Toffler, *Future Shock* (New York: Random House, 1970).

7. INTERGOVERNMENTAL RELATIONS

1. Robert L. Lineberry and Ira Sharkansky, *Urban Politics and Public Policy* (New York: Harper & Row, 1971), pp. 114-15.

2. This principle is known as Dillon's Rule. See John F. Dillon, *Commentaries on the Law of Municipal Corporations*, 5th ed. (Boston: 1911), 1: 448.

3. Wallace S. Sayre and Herbert Kaufman, *Governing New York City* (New York: Russell Sage, 1960), pp. 564-82.

4. *See* Raymond A. Wolfinger, *The Politics of Progress* (Englewood Cliffs, N.J.: Prentice-Hall, forthcoming), chap. 9.

5. Deil S. Wright, "Intergovernmental Relations in Large Council-Manager Cities," unpublished paper, October 1970, p. 13.

6. *See* Alan K. Campbell, ed., *The States and the Urban Crisis* (Englewood Cliffs, N.J.: Prentice-Hall, 1970).

7. Wright, "Intergovernmental Relations," pp. 27-29; and A. Lee Fritschler, B. Douglas Harman, and Morley Segal, "Federal, State, Local Relationships," *Urban Data Service* (December 1969), pp. 4-5.

8. *See* Martha Derthick, "Intercity Differences in Administration of the Public Assistance Program: The Case of Massachusetts," in James Q. Wilson, ed., *City Politics and Public Policy* (New York: Wiley, 1968), p. 264.

9. *See* Gilbert Y. Steiner, *The State of Welfare* (Washington, D.C.: Brookings Institution, 1971).

10. Cf. Deil S. Wright, "The States and Intergovernmental Relations," *Publius* 1 (winter 1972): 37-38.

11. (Lexington, Ky.: Council of State Governments). An examination of p. 9-10 of the second paper indicates that the problem is perhaps exaggerated somewhat. In any case the authors of the paper admit that it is very difficult to determine accurately the cost of federal red tape.

12. Morton Grodzins, *The American System* (Chicago: Rand McNally, 1966), p. 11. For further refinements of the Grodzins thesis, *see* Morley Segal and A. Lee Fritschler, "Policy Making in the Intergovernmental System, *Publius* 1 (winter 1972): 95-122; and Deil S. Wright, "Intergovernmental Relations," paper prepared for the Conference on Federalism, Duke University, 21 January 1972.

13. Grodzins, *The American System*, p. 80.

14. Ibid., pp. 75-80.

15. Ibid., pp. 150-51.

16. Douglas St. Angelo, "Formal and Routine Local Control of National Programs," in Daniel J. Elazar et al., eds., *Cooperation and Conflict: Readings in American Federalism* (Itasca, Ill.: Peacock, 1969), pp. 442-52.

17. Cf. Thomas J. Anton, "Roles and Symbols in the Determination of State Expenditures," *Midwest Journal of Political Science* 11 (February 1967): 37-38; and Deil S. Wright, "Executive Manpower for Indeterminate Government: Staffing the States" (Paper delivered at the National Conference of the American Society for Public Administration, New York, 1972). Anton concludes that the "states have lost effective control over their expenditures," while Wright argues that "intergovernmental fiscal demands have consumed almost all the 1958-1970 increase in state tax revenues."

18. The income tax is a superior means of assuring that revenue keeps pace with economic growth. *See* Advisory Commission on Intergovernmental Relations, *Revenue Sharing—An Idea Whose Time Has Come* (Washington, D.C.: Government Printing Office, 1970), pp. 3-4.

19. Cf. Joseph A. Doorley, "The Art of Grantsmanship," in Douglas M. Fox, ed., *The New Urban Politics: Cities and the Federal Government* (Pacific Palisades, Ca.:

Goodyear, 1972), pp. 90-92; and Russell D. Murphy, *Political Entrepreneurs and Urban Poverty* (Lexington, Mass.: Heath, 1971), pp. 53-54, 63-64.

20. Campbell, *The States and the Urban Crisis,* p. 25. In the early 1970s the federal revenue "surplus" vanished while state-local revenues went increasingly into the black. Whether this new trend will persist is unclear.

21. These tables are derived from *Governmental Finances in 1968-69* (Washington, D.C.: Government Printing Office, 1970), pp. 2, 31.

22. This typology is taken from Daniel J. Elazar, *American Federalism* (New York: Crowell, 1966), p. 70.

23. *See* Derthick, *Differences in Administration of Assistance Programs,* p. 6, for a useful way of distinguishing among the types of grants described in the following paragraphs.

24. *See* Advisory Commission on Intergovernmental Relations, *Revenue Sharing,* p. 8.

25. Daniel J. Elazar, "Fiscal Questions and Political Answers in Intergovernmental Finance," *Public Administration Review* 21 (September-October 1972): 476.

26. *See* Wright, "Executive Manpower for Indeterminate Government," pp. 5-6.

27. Wright, "The States and Intergovernmental Relations," p. 22.

28. Ibid., pp. 16-17.

29. Burton D. Friedman and Laird J. Dunbar, *Grants Management in Education: Federal Impact on State Agencies* (Chicago: Public Administration Service, 1971), p. 20.

30. Senate Subcommittee on Intergovernmental Relations, Committee on Government Operations, "The Federal System as Seen by Local Officials" (Washington, D.C.: Government Printing Office, 1963), p. 44.

31. Senate Subcommittee on Intergovernmental Relations, Committee on Government Operations, "The Federal System as Seen by Federal Aid Officials" (Washington, D.C.: Government Printing Office, 1965), p. 53.

32. *See* Terry Sanford, *Storm over the States* (New York: McGraw-Hill, 1967); and "Federal Grant-in-Aid Requirements" (Lexington, Ky.: Council of State Governments), pp. 7-10.

33. Harold Seidman, *Politics, Position and Power* (New York: Oxford University Press, 1970), pp. 138ff.

34. Senate Subcommittee on Intergovernmental Relations, Committee on Government Operations, "The Federal System as Seen by Federal Aid Officials," p. 55.

35. Nancy N. Anderson, "The Governor and Comprehensive Health Planning," in Thad L. Beyle and Oliver P. Williams, eds., *The American Governor in Behavioral Perspective* (New York: Harper & Row, 1972), p. 221.

36. House Committee on Government Operations, "The Bloc Grant Programs of the Law Enforcement Assistance Administration," pt. 2 (Washington, D.C.: Government Printing Office, 1971), p. 722.

37. Ibid., pp. 494-95.

8. THE POLITICS OF BUDGETING

1. Leonard D. White, *Trends in Public Administration* (New York: McGraw-Hill, 1933), pp. 207-8.

2. *See* Jane S. Dahlberg, *The New York Bureau of Municipal Research* (New York: New York University Press, 1966), pp. 176-82.

3. Allen Schick, *Budget Innovation in the States* (Washington, D.C.: Brookings Institution, 1971), p. 57.

4. Ibid., pp. 8-10. It should be pointed out that other writers have employed different concepts of the two budgetary systems. *See* Robert Scott Gilmour, *Chang-*

ing Political Needs and the Budgetary Process in Florida (Gainesville: Public Administration Clearing Service, University of Florida, 1964), pp. 24-27.

5. *See* Stanley B. Botner, "Four Years of PPBS: An Appraisal," *Public Administration Review* 30 (July-August 1970): 423-31; and "PPB Under Nixon," *Public Administration Review* 32 (May-June 1972): 254-55.

6. Schick, op. cit., p. 1.

7. Ibid., pp. 4-5.

8. *See* Gilmour, *Changing Political Needs*, pp. 28-38; and "A PPB System," *Proceedings of the Academy of Political Science* 28 (January 1967): 189.

9. *See* Botner, "Four Years of PPBS," and Aaron Wildavsky and Arthur Hammond, "Comprehensive Versus Incremental Budgeting in the Department of Agriculture," *Administrative Science Quarterly* 10 (1965): 321-46. I also base this statement on conversation with state budget agency officials.

10. J. Terry Edwards and E. Lester Levine, "Departments and Innovation: The Response to PPBS in Florida" (Paper delivered at the Annual Meeting of the American Society for Public Administration, Denver, 1971), pp. 17-25; and interviews with officials of state central budgets office, as well as state and city educators.

11. Botner, "A PPB System."

12. *See* James David Barber, *Power in Committees: An Experiment in the Governmental Process* (Chicago: Rand McNally, 1966), pp. 37-38.

13. Preauditing is the inspection of an agency's spending plans before expenditures are allotted to the agency. Post-auditing is the inspection of an agency's spending records after it has spent the money allotted.

14. The preceding section is based on George A. Bell, "Budgeting in State Government," *State Government* (autumn 1967), pp. 231-38. *See also Budgeting by the States* (Lexington, Ky.: Council of State Governments, 1967).

15. This section is based primarily on Thomas J. Anton, "Roles and Symbols in the Determination of State Expenditures," *Midwest Journal of Political Science* 11 (February 1967): 27-43.

16. Deil S. Wright, "Executive Leadership in State Administration," *Midwest Journal of Political Science* 11 (February 1967): 18. *See also* Rufus P. Browning, "Innovative and Non-Innovative Decision Processes in Government Budgeting," in Robert T. Golembiewski, ed., *Public Budgeting and Finance* (Itasca, Ill.: Peacock, 1968), pp. 128-45; and Gerald E. Sullivan, "Incremental Budget-Making in the American States," *Journal of Politics* 34 (May 1972): 639-48.

17. Deil S. Wright, "Executive Manpower for Indeterminate Government: Staffing the States" (Paper delivered at the National Conference of the American Society for Public Administration, New York, 1972), p. 10.

18. Cf. Robert A. Dahl and Charles E. Lindblom, *Politics, Economics, and Welfare* (New York: Harper, 1953), pp. 254-55.

19. Allen Schick, "Control Patterns in State Budget Execution," *Public Administration Review* 24 (1964): 99.

20. Ira Sharkansky, "Agency Requests, Gubernatorial Support, and Budget Success in State Legislatures," *American Political Science Review* 62 (December 1968): 1220-31.

21. Ira Sharkansky and Augustus B. Turnbull, III, "Budget-making in Georgia and Wisconsin: A Test of a Model," in Ira Sharkansky, ed., *Policy Analysis in Political Science* (Chicago: Markham, 1970), pp. 225-37. They found that deviations from this pattern occur when (1) the governor is motivated to support agencies' requests to the point of overlooking budget "padding"; (2) both the governor and legislature realize that a tax increase is inevitable, and they accept agency requests as a means of justifying the increase to the public; (3) the governor strongly supports a program and is able to win the legislature's cooperation; (4) the governor and legislature are willing to permit major growth for an agency whose responsibilities have been in-

creased by a major new program; (5) nonbudgeting conflicts between the governor and legislature are carried over into budgeting and make the legislature less willing to accede to budget recommendations; and (6) there is a predisposition by the governor and legislature against agencies dealing with taxation, law enforcement, or economic regulation.

22. John P. Crecine, *Governmental Problem-Solving: A Computer Simulation of Municipal Budgeting* (Chicago: Rand McNally, 1969), p. 39.

23. Ibid., p. 74.

24. Ibid., p. 218. Cf. Arnold J. Meltsner, *The Politics of City Revenue* (Berkeley: University of California Press, 1971), pp. 181-84.

25. David A. Caputo, "Normative and Empirical Implications of Budgetary Process" (Paper delivered at the Annual Meeting of the American Political Science Association, New York, 1970), pp. 15-16.

26. Robert Eyestone, *The Threads of Public Policy: A Study in Policy Leadership* (Indianapolis: Bobbs-Merrill, 1971), p. 95.

27. Deil S. Wright, "The Dynamics of Budgeting—Large Council-Manager Cities," unpublished paper, 1969, pp. 22-24.

28. Crecine, *Governmental Problem-Solving*, p. 52.

29. Caputo, "Implications of Budgetary Process," p. 13.

30. Meltsner, *The Politics of City Revenue*, pp. 177-79.

31. F. Gerald Brown and Thomas P. Murphy, *Emerging Patterns in Urban Administration* (Lexington, Mass.: Heath, 1970), p. 17.

32. York Willbern, "Personnel and Money," in James W. Fesler, ed., *The 50 States and Their Local Communities* (New York: Knopf, 1967), p. 369.

33. *See* Dennis D. Riley, "Party Competition and State Policy Making: The Need for a Reexamination," *Western Political Quarterly* 24 (September 1971): 510-13, for a discussion of the appropriateness of this type of research for the testing of a series of propositions not examined here.

34. "The Politics of Redistribution," *American Political Science Review* 64 (June 1970): 522.

35. "The Literature Dealing with the Relationships Between Political Processes, Socioeconomic Conditions, and Public Policies in the American States: A Bibliographical Essay," *Polity* 1: 404.

36. "Executive Power and Public Policy in the States," *Western Political Quarterly* 22 (December 1969): 926-39.

37. Robert L. Lineberry and Edmund P. Fowler, "Reformism and Public Policies in American Cities," *American Political Science Review* 61 (September 1967): 701-16.

38. Raymond E. Wolfinger and John Osgood Field, "Political Ethos and the Structure of City Government," *American Political Science Review* 60 (June 1966): 306-26; and Robert L. Lineberry, "Community Structure and Planning Commitment: A Note on the Correlates of Agency Expenditures," *Social Science Quarterly* 50 (December 1969): 723-30.

9. BUREAUCRACY AND THE PUBLIC

1. James Q. Wilson, "The Bureaucracy Problem," *Public Interest* 6 (winter 1967): 3-9. The next three paragraphs are based on this article.

2. Charles A. Reich, *The Greening of America* (New York: Random House, 1970), pp. 103-9.

3. Gideon Sjoberg et al., "Bureaucracy and the Lower Class," *Sociology and Social Research* 50 (April 1966): 325-37.

4. Michael Lipsky, *Protest in City Politics: Rent Strikes, Housing, and the Power of the Poor* (Chicago: Rand McNally, 1970), p. 94.

5. Michael Parenti, "Power and Pluralism: A View from the Bottom," *Journal of Politics* 32 (August 1970): 511-12. *See also* Harold V. Savitch, "Powerlessness in an Urban Ghetto," *Polity* 5 (fall 1972): 19-56.

6. Sjoberg, "Bureaucracy and the Lower Class."

7. Two excellent essays by Herbert Kaufman place these developments in historical perspective: "Emerging Conflicts in the Doctrines of Public Administration," *American Political Science Review* 50 (December 1956): 1057-73; and "Administrative Decentralization and Political Power," *Public Administration Review* 29 (January-February 1969): 3-15.

8. "Ombudsman" is a Swedish word meaning agent, representative, or deputy. As one might surmise, the office of ombudsman, as it is known today, originated in Scandinavia.

9. *See* "In 5 States, Ombudsmen Spur Aid to Citizens," *New York Times*, 10 May 1972, p. 10.

10. *See* Alan A. Altshuler, *Community Control: The Black Demand for Participation in Large American Cities* (New York: Pegasus, 1970); and Joseph F. Zimmerman, *The Federated City* (New York: St. Martin's, 1972), for a discussion of the issues involved in community control.

11. *See* Claire W. Gilbert, "The Study of Community Power," in Scott Greer et al., eds., *The New Urbanization* (New York: St. Martin's, 1968), pp. 228-30; and Wallace S. Sayre, "Smaller Does Not Mean Better, Necessarily," *New York Times*, 8 April 1972, p. 35.

12. Cf. Sayre, "Smaller Does Not Mean Better, Necessarily."

13. Irving Kristol, "Decentralization for What?" *Public Interest* 11 (spring 1968): 17-25.

14. Emanuel Perlmutter, "Decentralization of Schools Fails, Kenneth Clark Says," *New York Times*, 9 May 1972, p. 1.

15. *See* Harold Seidman, "Crisis of Confidence in Government," *Political Quarterly* 43 (January-March 1972): 85-86; and Douglas M. Fox, "The President's Proposals for Executive Reorganization: A Critique," *Public Administration Review* 33 (September-October 1973).

16. *See* Wilson, "The Bureaucracy Problem"; Robert Wood, "When Government Works," *Public Interest* 18 (November 1970); and Peter Woll, "Administrative Law in the Seventies," *Public Administration Review* 32 (September-October 1972): 564.

17. *See* Alice M. Rivlin, *Systematic Thinking for Social Action* (Washington, D.C.: Brookings Institution, 1971); and "Why Can't We Get Things Done?" *Brookings Bulletin* 9, no. 2 (1972): 5-9.

18. *See* Frances Fox Piven and Richard A. Cloward, *Regulating the Poor* (New York: Pantheon, 1971), pp. 320-38.

19. *See* Paul Davidoff, "Advocacy and Pluralism in Planning," *Journal of the American Institute of Planners* 31 (November 1965): 333-38.

20. *See* Frank Marini, ed., *Toward a New Public Administration* (San Francisco: Chandler, 1971).

Index

state legislature, 39-40
California Supreme Court, property tax
support of schools and, 44
Categorical grants, 79-84
Chicago, Ill., 9, 32, 35, 49
patronage employees in, 17
Chief executives, 4. *See also* City
Manager, Governor, Mayor
Citizens Committee for Children, 56
Citizens Conference on State Legislatures, 39
City government, 16-18. *See also*
Mayor
federal grants as source of revenue
for, 76-80
federal relations with, 74-76, 80-82
federal revenue sharing and, 82-84
fragmentation of, 16-17
state influence on, 72-74
City manager
policy development and, 33-34
policy implementation and, 36
resources of, 34
Civil service, 6, 13-14, 80. *See also*
Merit system
city size and, 52
coverage in cities, 17-18
governor's personnel powers and, 28
Civil service commission, 18
Clark, Joseph, 32
Clark, Kenneth, 100
Cleveland, Ohio, 32, 65, 93, 94
Clientele, bureau, 55
Collective bargaining, 61, 63. *See also*
Government employee unions;
Strikes; *and* Unions
Common Cause, 102-03
Common Sense Associates, 56
Communications media, 64-68
elite, 64
executive branch and, 64-65
government official versus, 65-66
mass, 64
electronic, 64
printed, 64
policy development and, 66-67
policy implementation and, 67-68
trouble-shooting role of, 68
Connecticut, 11, 27, 41, 43, 58. *See
also* New Haven
Consultants
management, 70
institutes, 70
profit-making, 70
substantive issue, 69-70
Conventions, national political (1972),
9
Corning, Erastus, 52
Costikyan, Edward, 21

"Cost to the states resulting from delays
in authorization or appropriation
of federal grants-in-aid," 75
Council of Chief State School Officers,
82
Council of State Governments, 70, 75
Counties, 16
Courts, 43-46
administrative, 44
policy development and, 44-45
policy implementation and, 45-46

Daley, Richard, 32, 35, 53
Decentralization, 99-100
in antipoverty program, 99
costs of, 100
in New York city schools, 100
in public education, 62, 99
Department, 3-4
fire, 9-10
police, 9, 14
Department of Health, Education, and
Welfare, 81
Department of Social Services, 81
Detroit, Mich., 17, 31, 65, 93-94
Dilworth, Richardson, 32
Districts
school, 16
special, 16-17
Division of Vocational Rehabilitation, 81
Domestic programs, 77
Doorley, Joseph, 32

Education, 76, 79, 83. *See also* schools
Efficiency, 97
Election, nonpartisan, 48-49
Equity, 97
Evader, 32
Evans, Rowland, 65
Expenditure patterns, factors associated
with, 96

"Federal Grant-in-Aid Requirements
Impeding State Administration,"
75
Fire department, firemen, 9, 63
Fiscal integrity, 97
Flat grants, 77-78
Florida, 40, 76, 84, 89, 91. *See also*
Miami, *and* Miami Beach
Florida Department of Veterans'
Affairs, 56
"Flower fund," 51
Formula grants, 78
Fragmentation
in city government, 16-17